The Mountain Meitheal Handbook Of Trail Design and Construction

2011

Bill Murphy

GET OUT, GET DIRTY, GIVE BACK.

Mountain Meitheal
www.pathsavers.org

coillte

Published by Mountain Meitheal with the financial support of Coillte.

Published by Mountain Meitheal
© Mountain Meitheal and Bill Murphy 2011

ISBN 978-0-9568452-0-7

Ballyhoura Development Ltd financially supported the first edition of this handbook in 2006.

THE NATIONAL TRAILS OFFICE ENDORSES THIS BOOK.

CREDITS AND ACKNOWLEDGEMENTS
Thanks are due to Shay Walsh and Clíona Ní Bhréartúin for editing, helpful comments and proof reading the text. Special thanks to Tom Byrne and Coillte for their generous support for this book.

Original text, sketches, diagrams and photographs by the author with additional photographs by Shay Walsh (Mountain Meitheal) and Daithí de Forge (Coillte Recreation Team) and Martin Ruane (Coillte Recreation Team).

FURTHER COPIES OF THIS BOOK AND INFORMATION ON THE WORK OF MOUNTAIN MEITHEAL IS AVAILABLE THROUGH THE WEBSITE WWW.PATHSAVERS.ORG

FOR MORE INFORMATION ON A VARIETY OF TRAILS AND OUTDOOR RECREATION IN IRELAND SEE WWW.COILLTEOUTDOORS.IE

Table of Contents

This book is dedicated to the memory of two Mountain Meitheal members who sadly passed away in 2011

Joss Lynam
Mountaineer, outdoorsman and trail advocate.

Joss was a legendary figure in the outdoor community, a skilled alpinist and mountaineer. He was a strong advocate for the use of our mountains and wild places for outdoor recreation and a founder of AFAS. He devoted many years service to the outdoor community through his involvement in Mountaineering Ireland, and was often the voice of compromise and reason as the Mountaineering Ireland representative at Comhairle na Tuaithe. As Chairman of the National Trails Advisory Committee he was a keen promoter of the value of trails. Joss was one of Mountain Meitheal's earliest members and always supported our work - if not in person, certainly in spirit. Joss blazed the trail for others to follow.

Angela Sweeney
Trail volunteer, outdoorswoman and friend

Angela was a stalwart member of Mountain Meitheal for many years until her untimely death in 2011. She served on the committee and was the embodiment of the true spirit of volunteering. She will be remembered for her unique sense of humour, her organisational skills and her unflinching dedication to the protection of the environment. On workdays she laboured with an enthusiasm and gusto that inspired those around her. Her fun, spirit of the outdoors and enthusiasm will be sorely missed.

> THE WOODS ARE LOVELY, DARK AND DEEP,
>
> BUT I HAVE PROMISES TO KEEP,
>
> AND MILES TO GO BEFORE I SLEEP,
>
> AND MILES TO GO BEFORE I SLEEP.
>
> ROBERT FROST

PREFACE

There is a huge increase in the number of people wanting to get out and enjoy the outdoors. This is to be welcomed as all the research shows that this benefits the nation's health and well being and, in difficult times, increases our ability to cope with the day to day challenges we all face. Interestingly we are also seeing an increase in the numbers of people who want to spend part of their time to make the outdoors a better place to visit. Mountain Meitheal has been a pioneer in this area for close to ten years. Coillte is delighted to be associated with Mountain Meitheal and values the contribution that all its members make to the nations recreation infrastructure. Mountain Meitheal's work is important in helping Coillte to reach one of our key goals – attracting people to nature and supporting local communities.

Recreation is one of the important public goods that Coillte provides. However, as with all human activities, recreation is not with out it's own impact. These impacts are all too evident and the sustainable management and use of our trails should concern all of us. Coillte congratulates Mountain Meitheal on the publication of the second edition of this important handbook for the outdoor community in Ireland. This book contributes to the sustainable management of the earth's natural resources and raises awareness of sustainable recreation.

As the largest provider of outdoor recreation in Ireland, Coillte strives to provide sustainable, enjoyable and authentic recreation experiences. This book will be an important contribution to reaching that goal while attracting people to nature.

David Gunning

Chief Executive, Coillte.

1. INTRODUCTION

WHY TRAILS?

In recent years, there has been a huge increase in the number of people taking to the outdoors to enjoy the fresh air, the scenery, the solitude and the challenge Ireland's mountains, forests and wild lands have to offer. For the most part this is to be welcomed; however, it is increasing the pressures on what are often very sensitive landscapes.

Trails are fundamental to the way people access the countryside for outdoor recreation and how they perceive their surroundings. Correctly designed and constructed trails 'guide' people in the outdoors allowing them to access different landscapes and recreation experiences. Given the ever-increasing demands for outdoor activities, trails are a valuable tool for land managers to provide access in a more sustainable way. Outdoor enthusiasts, including walkers, hikers, mountain bikers, horse riders and motorised users among others, compete for what is a finite resource. Many of Ireland's trails and routes have not been designed and constructed, but have developed through use along desire lines. Added to this, Ireland has high rainfall and wet peaty soils in many of the areas where people choose to walk (and mountain bike) with the result that many of our 'trails' and landscapes are increasingly showing the impact of this extra recreational use. As a result trails are eroded and hillsides scarred.

1 UPLAND EROSION IN THE WICKLOW MOUNTAINS CAUSED BY FEET

WHAT CAUSES THE EROSION?

More feet mean more trampling and more tyres mean more dragging (caused by skidding) of the vegetation[1] in vulnerable upland landscapes. Due to a combination of the harsher climate and the nutritionally poorer soils in the uplands, vegetation is slow to recover when damaged. Vegetation on or close to 'trails' will eventually die with this continuous damage and the roots that bind the soil together will cease to perform that task. In Ireland this exposed soil is often peat. Peat is very prone to erosion by rain and wind. When wet, peat sticks to boots and tyres and is carried away by water – when dry, it blows away easily. After a relatively short period with no vegetation to bind it together exposed soil will rut, gullies will form and scars on the mountains quickly become evident. (See Figure1)

DO WE NEED TRAIL MAINTENANCE? SHOULD WE BE BUILDING TRAILS IN WILD AREAS?

It has been argued that we should not intervene in the wild environment. It has been suggested that our uplands are wild and that building trails and paths only make the mountains less wild and

---

1 Heather (*Calluna vulgaris*) is the common ground cover in our uplands. This is a woody plant which when damaged breaks and does not regenerate easily without the intervention of fire.

encourages more users into these landscapes. In an ideal world this would be true. However, look around any heavily used wild landscape in Ireland and the impacts of OUR feet and OUR wheels are very obvious on these beautiful and sensitive areas.

The old maxim – *take only photos, leave only footprints* – is just not good enough anymore. The reality is **we are leaving too many footprints**. Trails help to manage and reduce our impact. Trails provide a durable surface while protecting the surrounding environment. We in Mountain Meitheal believe that path maintenance and building is a way to limit the impact to smaller areas – the trail corridor – thereby protecting the mountain environment and is the lesser of two evils.

Trail building in mountain and remote areas should not be about making the experience easier or less challenging but about landscape and environmental protection. (See Our Objectives.) Good trail building in remote areas and in sensitive landscapes should be difficult to see; it should blend with the landscape using good design features and where possible locally sourced materials.

TRAIL BUILDING MORE THAN WAY-MARKING

In recent years we have seen many 'trails' developed across the country. While local groups have put considerable effort into the initial development, negotiating access, installing stiles, bridges, way-marking etc. there has often been little consideration to the actual structure of the **trail tread**. This is understandable given that little was known when these trails were being laid out about the impact that humans can leave on a landscape even through walking. Many of these routes unfortunately are now showing the signs of heavy use and of less than perfect initial route selection and design.

This booklet is designed to introduce trail managers, builders, maintainers and promoters to some of the basic skills and techniques required to develop and maintain sustainable trails in Ireland. The expertise gained by Mountain Meitheal over the past ten years and its contact with overseas trail workers and organisations form the basis of this publication. It endeavours to bring this expertise and experience together in one book to present a useful guide that deals with trails under Irish conditions.

MOUNTAIN MEITHEAL OBJECTIVES

To protect and conserve the mountain and forest environment by repairing, maintaining and building mountain and forest trails while

- Maintaining the challenge for recreational users and
- Striving to preserve a sense of solitude and a 'wilderness' experience.

To spread an awareness of sustainable recreation.

To provide enjoyable projects and activities for its volunteers.

2. SAFETY

SAFETY IS EVERYONE'S RESPONSIBILITY

Whether it's hiking, cycling or repairing trails all mountain activity presents some hazards. Mountains can be dangerous places as the weather can change quickly making conditions under foot dangerous. People can also get cold and wet. Add swinging a mattock to the mix and it is evident that trail work can be dangerous. When working on a trail, safety must be everyone's first concern.

TOOL TALK

Crew leaders should begin each day's work with a brief safety talk pointing out:
- Potential hazards
- Safe work practices and
- The work of the day.

All crew members need to pay special attention to this talk and should familiarise themselves with the hazard identification sheet (Figure 2) which should be posted on site by the crew leader.

HAZARD IDENTIFICATION

The crew leader or the project manager should complete a hazard identification form and this should be posted at the work site for all crew members to see. List the hazards, the possible injury, the action required to avoid injury and list special equipment. The following is a list (Table 1) that can be used as a guide to establishing hazards. **It is not an exhaustive list.**

TABLE 1 POTENTIAL SAFETY HAZARDS IN TRAIL WORK

Hazard	Possible resulting injury	Action to avoid injury	Equipment
Cold wet weather	Hypothermia	Ensure proper outdoor equipment, warm drink and snack	Waterproof outer wear, boots, hat, fleeces etc.
Hot Sun	Heat Exhaustion Dehydration Sun burn	Ensure people drink plenty of water and use sun protection and / or a hat and neckerchief.	Sun screen, broad brimmed hat, water bottles.
Flying stone or chips	Eye injury	Wear eye goggles and stand clear of people using sledges, picks etc.	Eye goggles
Uneven or slippery ground	Slips, trips and falls	Wear appropriate footwear. Ensure clear ground when working	Proper mountain boots
Hitting a co-worker with tools	Serious injury to any part of body	Ensure safe working distance – see below	
Saws, axes and secateurs	Cuts, scratches, nicks	Wear work gloves and eye protection working in woods	Gloves / eye protection
Crow bars	Crushing fingers, feet	Keep fingers and feet away from crow bars or other tools used to prise rocks or other heavy weights	Gloves and heavy boots

Ticks	Lyme disease	Avoid short sleeves/trousers when working in deep vegetation. Apply insect repellent, check after work	Long sleeved shirt, long pants, insect repellent
Bees/wasps	Stings	Mark out hives and avoid working in that area	
Heavy weights	Back injury	Learn appropriate lifting techniques. Get help when lifting. Use a lever or winch	
Winch	Wire snap	Use only correct equipment – handle etc. Check before use. Establish safe working area	Correct equipment and replacement parts only should be used.
Pegs on trees/ branches	Eye injury	Wear work gloves and eye protection working in woods	Gloves / eye protection

2. EXAMPLE OF HAZARD IDENTIFICATION FORM

BASIC SAFETY RULES

Safety is primarily common sense, but as some one once noted 'common sense is not as common as we think' therefore here are some basic safety rules.

Heed all safety instructions of crew leaders. They are there to make your day as enjoyable, productive and safe as possible. You can help by following all safety advice. If you don't know, ask.

One leader, one voice. The leader is in charge, please respect their instructions.

Have a first aid kit to hand. Ensure that there is a fully stocked first aid kit to hand and that some one knows how to use it.

Don't use unfamiliar tools without training. If you don't know how to use a tool, ask for help.

SAFE WORKING DISTANCE
2 x HANDLES

3 SAFE WORKING DISTANCE

Make sure **all tools are sharp**, have sound handles and that the heads are tight.
Checking tools before you start is important. Don't use faulty or blunt tools – it's only harder work for you and can be dangerous.

Don't use power tools without proper training and safety procedures. **Tools like chain saws and volunteers don't mix.** You will need a certificate of competence to use a chain saw. Check the club rules regarding chain saws.

4 BEND YOUR KNEES WHEN LIFTING

Ensure a safe working distance from others. (Figure 3)

Don't work alone. Working alone can be very dangerous particularly in mountainous areas. If marking a trail on the ground on your own always let someone know where you are and your return time.

Do not work in heavy rain. When gloves, tools and materials are sodden, the danger of accidents occurring increases. Sloping ground becomes more hazardous and can cause slips.

Ensure you have the proper personal equipment for working in the mountains. Bring sufficient food, a warm drink and suitable clothing.

Always wear work gloves (and eye protection when working in the woods.)

When moving heavy weights, **bend you knees** and use your leg muscles, not your back muscles. (Figure 4.) Ideally get help when lifting.

Warm up and cool down before and after working with some stretching exercises.

Don't leave tools lying around as trip hazards. Take care with all tools and store them off the trail when not in use to avoid tripping other volunteers or passers by.

Don't leave the worksite in an unsafe state. The crew leader should walk the day's work to ensure that the trail is in safe condition for other users. Remove any loose rocks, branches and tripping hazards etc. Ensure borrow pits are made safe.

Erect warning signs at the beginning of each day warning other users of your on-going work.

INSURANCE
Before you begin your work you will need to consider the issue of insurance. Different trail organisations use different approaches but it is essential that you arrange for some insurance cover. Many state landowners and managers will want to see that your club's insurance policy indemnifies them from claims arising from injuries that might occur to your volunteers.

Mountaineering Ireland has added trail work to the list of activities covered under their general insurance policy. If you are a club, check with Mountaineering Ireland to see if you are covered under their insurance. A club may also want to get additional insurance and any good insurance broker will be able to advise on this. It is important to emphasise the true nature of the work – digging, ground works etc. – to the insurance broker and that no power tools will be used.

Insurance is not overly expensive and is well worth having.

OUR BEST ADVICE IS TO GET GOOD ADVICE.

3. TRAIL DESIGN, PLANNING AND LAYOUT

PLANNING A TRAIL

As trails are fundamental to the way people access the countryside and how they perceive their surroundings, well-designed trails are essential to 'guide' people in the outdoors, providing them with an authentic recreation experience. For trail managers, good trail systems allow land managers to 'control' where people should and should not go (**positive** and **negative control points**). Well-constructed trails ensure that erosion is reduced or avoided by removing water off the trail and keeping people on durable and sustainable surfaces. Trail design, therefore, encompasses everything from initial route selection and trail corridor layout to the actual treadway design and material choice. All these elements are essential in developing a sustainable trail network.

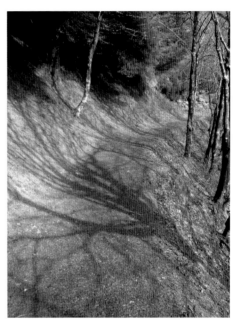

If a recreation trail user is given an <u>authentic recreation experience</u> on a well-designed and built trail, they will generally stay on the trail. Trail design is the single most important factor in determining recreation experience and therefore the long-term durability of any trail.

Good trail design will:
- Minimize maintenance
- Provide a more enjoyable and authentic trail experience for users and
- Reduce construction costs (by, for example, avoiding wet areas).

Poor design and trail layout often results in trails that are unsustainable because:
- There is soil erosion and poor underfoot conditions,
- People are not keeping to trails and 'off trail' pressures are occurring along the trail because the trail lacks interest,

These trails become expensive to manage and maintain and therefore easily fall into disrepair.

5 A BENCH CUT TRAIL.
This bench cut trail provides a durable solution on this steep slope by contouring along the slope and allowing water to sheet across the trail without causing erosion.

WHAT IS A SUSTAINABLE TRAIL?

Sustainable trails.....
...... **guide users** to positive control points and avoid negative control points.
A sustainable trail will lead users to desired destinations such as bridges and road crossings, historic sites, viewpoints and vistas, interesting landforms and user facilities - camp sites, picnic areas etc. - while avoiding wet areas, steep slopes, critical habitats, and other culturally or environmentally sensitive areas.

.......**keep water off the trail**. Water erosion is the number one problem for sustainable trails. It damages trails, is expensive to repair and diminishes the user's experience. In Ireland, water is the primary erosive force. Trails that collect water or channel water will be both environmentally and economically unsustainable.

......**keep users on the trail** and provide an authentic experience. Users leave the trail when it is eroded, excessively wet, or when the trail does not meet their needs or expectations. When users leave the trail tread, they widen it; this creates braided and unsustainable bootleg trails. These can cause further environmental damage and raise maintenance costs. Sustainable trails must meet different users' needs and expectations. Ultimately, a sustainable trail design will be a trail that connects desired control points.

CONTROL POINTS

In designing a trail, the trail designer must select the **positive** and **negative control points**. Control points are useful for establishing the basis of any trail network. **Positive control points** include vantage points, prominent rocks, safe river crossings and features such as picnic or camping sites etc that attract the user along the trail. **Negative control points** are features and areas the trail designer wants to steer people away from. These could include dangerous ledges, biodiversity or nature conservation sites (that would suffer from intrusion), wet areas that are difficult for trail management, important archaeological site, etc.

TABLE 2 CONTROL POINTS

POSITIVE CONTROL POINTS	NEGATIVE CONTROL POINTS
Scenic viewpoints	Environmentally sensitive sites that require protection
Visitor facilities such as car parks, bridges, designated camp sites and picnic locations, huts and shelters etc.	Private property where access is not allowed – houses, farmyards etc.
Robust cultural features – castles, sturdy megalithic monuments, standing stones etc.	Fragile man-made cultural artefacts – fragile megalithic monuments, old wallsteads etc.
Land forms – interesting rock outcrops or similar land forms	Gullies, steep side slopes (where trail construction will be costly and difficult to maintain)
Dry durable surfaces where trail construction will be easier	Low lying wet areas (where trail construction will be costly and difficult to maintain)
Safe road crossings or quite roads suitable for incorporation into route.	Dangerous features such as old mine shafts, quarries, cliffs, farmyards

Before starting any layout on the ground, plot the control points on a map. The control points are used as the basis for plotting the route of the trail on the ground.

USING CONTROL POINTS

Figure 6 illustrates how control points can aid trail design. Control Point **A** is the access point to the area and a positive control point. The trail network will start from this point. Control Point **D** is the end of the forest road; Control Point **F**, a river crossing; Control Point **G,** a national monument and point of interest; Control Point **H** is a possible connection point to an existing long distance route and Control Point **I** is the summit and a vantage point; all are positive control points. Any trail network should try and link these points. Control Point **B** is a sensitive biodiversity area where disturbance should be avoided; Control Point **C** is a quarry and a hazard to users and is also located on private land; Control Point **E** is a steep sided river gully that presents difficulties for river crossings. These are all negative control points that should be avoided when designing the trail corridor.

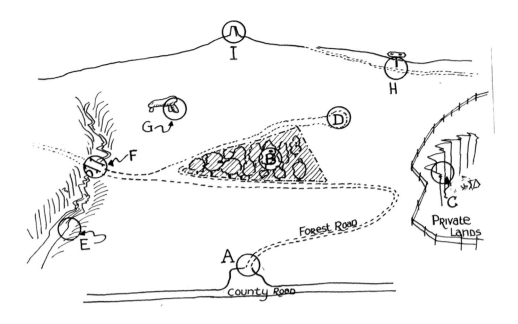

6 CONTROL POINTS

TRAIL NETWORKS

In designing a trail network it is important to consider the type of usage the trails will get. Figure 7 shows a number of possible trail layouts. From the trailhead (car park) adjacent to the county road the first trail type is a linear trail. Linear Trails are point-to-point trails offering the user a trail experience that starts and finishes in different location. Ireland's Wicklow Way is a good example of a linear trail.

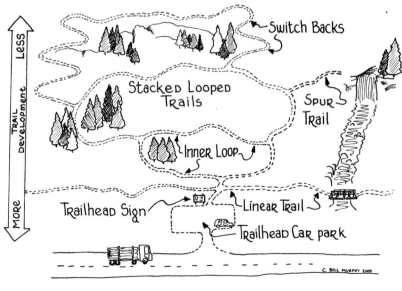

7 TRAIL SYSTEMS

Above, the linear trail in Figure 7 is a **stacked loop trail** system. This type of network is excellent for offering users differing levels of trail experience. The loops closest to the trailhead offer the easiest grade of trail for the user. As the trail system moves away from the car park, visitors can expect to experience more rugged and demanding trails. (Multi Access trails are best located on the inner loop of any stacked trail system).

The Ballyhoura Mountain Bike Trail network is a good example of a stacked loop system.

THE RIGHT TRAIL IN THE RIGHT PLACE

The objective in designing any trail is to put the right trail type into the right location. For example in an urban setting (Figure 8), trails for use by a jogger or a mum with a buggy or an elderly user will have a very different specification from an upland trail in a remote mountain environment (Figure 9).

Users in an urban park or close to a visitor centre have different requirements,

8 TRAILS IN AN URBAN SETTING.
Trails in an urban setting require a high level of engineering to ensure ease of use for a wide variety of casual users.

9 TRAILS IN A WILD LOCATION.
These need to be 'light on the landscape', using local materials and emphasising conservation over ease for the walker.

different skill levels and expectations and will use different equipment when on the trail than a hiker using a trail on a mountain.

The hill walker in Connemara would rightly consider that an asphalt path or overly wide or heavily engineered trail would take away from the wildness, scenic qualities and the challenge he or she seeks when visiting these wilder environments. The flip side of the coin is that gradients of over 5° make the use of a wheelchair or buggy quiet difficult, as do uneven surfaces, rustic waterbars or stone steps. Of course these are two opposite ends of the spectrum, but trail designers and managers need to give careful consideration to the type of trails that suit the landscape and usage.

Trail width, the materials and techniques used, gradients and the level of way-marking all have an impact on the recreation experience and need to be considered in trail design.

HOW DO WE DECIDE WHAT IS THE RIGHT TRAIL FOR THE RIGHT PLACE?

For recreational usage, Ireland can be classified under a number of recreational land types and each type will have a trail classification appropriate to the terrain. (Tables 3 & 4)

TABLE 3 WALKING TRAIL CLASSES SUITABLE FOR DIFFERENT TERRAIN TYPES

Land Type	Description	Class 1	Class 2	Class 3	Class 4	Class 5
Urban/ Urban Fringe	Cities, towns and villages and in urban and suburban parks	X	X			
Core Recreation Areas	Established recreational areas e.g. central areas of forest parks or national parks, near beach car parks, etc. forest areas	X	X	X		
Rural landscapes/ forests Areas within forest parks, national parks away from core areas	Countryside areas away from communities, villages, farmland and forest			X	X	
Upland or Remote area	Open mountain area, remote landscapes, areas far away from any habitation				X	X

While a **Class 1** walking trail (wide, smooth and flat) is appropriate for an urban park or near an interpretative centre it is not suitable for a long-distance route in a remote upland valley. Similarly, a **Class 5** off-road cycle trail (rugged with steep gradients and technically challenging) should not be located in a town park or close to areas of high use, e.g. forest park car-parks. (See the National Trail Classifications in appendix II and III).

TABLE 4 OFF-ROAD CYCLE TRAIL CLASSIFICATIONS

Land Type	Description	Class 1	Class 2	Class 3	Class 4	Class 5
Urban/ Urban Fringe	Cities, towns and villages and in urban and suburban parks	X	X			
Core Recreation Areas	Established recreational areas e.g. central areas of forest parks or national parks, near beach car parks, etc. forest areas	X	X	X		
Rural landscapes/ forests Areas within forest parks, national parks away from core areas	Countryside areas away from communities, villages; farmland and forest		X	X	X	
Upland or Remote area	Open mountain area, remote landscapes, areas far away from any habitation			X	X	X

By following the trail and land classification system, the trail provider ensures that trails are located where they are most suitable for the intended users and are appropriate and sympathetic to the environment.

SELECTING THE ROUTE

The old carpenter's adage of 'measure twice and cut once' should be applied to trail design and route selection. Before starting trail designers should scout the terrain well marking all the positive and negative control points as described above on a map of the area. Next mark the possible trail corridor on the map considering the control points, the topography, ground conditions and trail usage. It is then possible to go back on site and flag the outline corridor. Flagging the corridor will allow the trail designer to see the terrain of the proposed trail route and the different conditions that will need to be considered in construction.

During this planning phase the trail designer needs to consider:

THE TERRAIN

Examine closely the terrain through which the trail will pass. Pay particular attention to soil conditions, the topography and gradients. (See Appendix I. Gradients for use in Trail Construction). The positive and negative control points will be invaluable in assisting in avoiding problem areas at this stage.

VOLUME AND TYPE OF USAGE

Consider the volume of usage the trail is expected to carry – this will impact on construction methods and therefore will impact on the route chosen. Trails with higher usage levels will require higher levels of construction to cope with the higher volumes and will generally be wider and have fewer obstacles. As described above, selecting the right trail class for the right terrain is essential to good trail design. Trails in more remote areas will carry less traffic, users will generally be fitter, have higher skill levels, and therefore trails can be narrower, more rugged and more 'natural' in their appearance.

Consider also the type of usage. Depending on the type of usage, trails will have different specifications relating to the acceptable gradient for the trail and the materials and construction techniques that will be most appropriate. The target users, their fitness and skills level and the expected experience will all influence the level of construction required and therefore the route chosen.

The National Trails Office **trail standards,** which set out surfaces, widths etc. for trail construction in different terrain types in Ireland, should be your guide in trail class selection. (See Trail Classification Tables 3 & 4 and Appendices II and III)

EXPERIENCE

Decide on the experience that the trail is designed to give. For example a trail designed for fitness in developed parkland will have very different requirements from a hiking trail designed for an upland area where the users expect and want a challenge and to experience a sense of solitude and closeness to the natural world. In the urban situation the trail is secondary to the experience – the user wishes simply to exercise. In remote areas the trail is integral to the experience – an overly unnatural trail can destroy the experience.

SAFETY

The safety of users will be a consideration and the level of safety intervention will vary with trail type and terrain. By collecting the correct information for your control points (hazards are always negative control points) it will be possible to deal with hazards in a low impact way at the trail-planning phase.

TRAIL EFFICIENCY

Trail management and design is as much about psychology as it is about engineering and therefore is about managing people in an unobtrusive way. People want to use trails that are fun and **interesting** and **efficient**. Trail users don't want to feel they are putting a lot of effort in for nothing. This is where trail efficiency comes in.

Trail users like to be 'rewarded' by the efficient and interesting use of their efforts. For example, the trail designer is faced with getting a trail to the summit of a hill and wants to contour along the slope to avoid steep fall line trails, which will quickly erode and degrade. A switch back trail is an obvious solution. Tight switchbacks (Figure 10 below) could be seen by a hiker as inefficient – he or she knows that they could get to the summit faster by crossing the switch backs without leaving the tread too much. The trail user perceives the trail to be an inefficient use of his/her time. The curving switch backs – it still contours and is therefore sustainable – on the other hand does not allow for easy crossing and encourages the walker to stay on the trail. By using steps the trail designer can regain the height lost caused by using the wider curving switchbacks.

TiGHT SWITCH BACKS SEEN AS INEFFICIENT

BROAD SWITHBACKS WITH STEPS SEEM MORE EFFICIENT

10 TRAIL LAYOUT AND EFFICIENCY

11 THIS TRAIL GUIDES THE EYE ONWARDS WITH A SENSE OF DISCOVERY

SHAPES AND EDGES

When constructing trails we should aim for natural shapes – shapes that follow the landscape, add interest and encourage the user to go on. <u>Straight lines are not common in nature.</u> Natural shapes tend to be irregular or curving. The trail pictured in Figure 11 could easily have been constructed in a straight line however, by using a free flowing trail, the trail designer has managed to construct a more interesting trail that encourages the walker to 'explore' what is around the corner.

Trail edges can add enormously to the experience of the trail. Edges are often areas rich in views, flora and

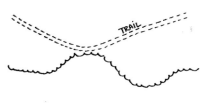

SKIRT EDGE AT ONE PLACE

19

fauna. Edges can be dealt with in a number of ways.

THE TRAIL TOUCHES THE EDGE AT ONE PLACE. This approach is used when we wish to give the trail user a view into a sensitive area (for example a bog land, sand dune or lake shore) but discourage entry.

THE TRAIL FOLLOWS THE BOUNDARY. Following the boundary prolongs the experience of being on the edge with the views and contrast that it brings.

CROSSING AN EDGE HEAD ON maximises the contrast between the two habitats that border the edge and provides a sudden change in perspective for the user.

CROSSING AN EDGE OBLIQUELY gives a more natural result than the 'head-on' approach.

CROSSING THE EDGE REPEATEDLY creates excitement and a sense of rapid progress.

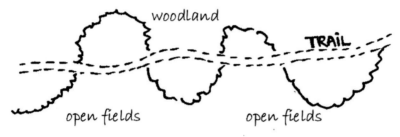

12 CROSSING AN EDGE REPEATEDLY CREATES A SENSE OF RAPID PROGRESS

CROSSING ROADS

In Ireland we have many road crossings to contend with and with ever increasing traffic they can present challenges for both safety and maintaining a good trail experience.

The best way to take a trail across a county road is 'head on' (See Figure 13-1) – this gets across the road in the shortest time – who really wants to walk on a busy road anyway? Select a site with good sight lines in both directions so hikers and drivers can see each other.

If the trail is not directly crossing the road consider bringing the trail across the road and run it parallel to the road but off the road – Figure 13-2.

Avoid going along the road if at all possible 13-3.

THE TRAIL CROSSINGS SHOULD BE SIGNPOSTED WELL FOR BOTH THE DRIVER AND THE WALKER.

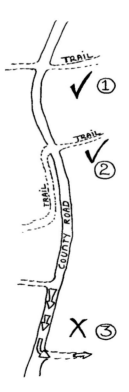

13 TRAIL/ROAD CROSSINGS

4. GETTING STARTED ON THE GROUND

DEALING WITH LANDOWNERS AND LAND MANAGERS AND GETTING PERMITS

The issue of access to the countryside in Ireland is a hugely contentious area but suffice to say that all land in Ireland belongs to some one or some organisation. Before commencing any trail work you will need to get permission from, or be invited in by, the landowners. The National Trails Office booklet – **Guidelines for developing and marking of way marked ways** – deals more extensively with the issue of permission from landowners.

SPECIAL AREAS OF CONSERVATION

Although you may set out with the objective of conserving the environment through developing a more sustainable trail network, some of your work maybe taking place in Special Areas of Conservation or similar habitat designations. If this is the case it is essential to get a licence from the local National Parks Service ranger. Generally they will advise you on what you can and cannot do. Explain your work plan and objectives and there will generally be no problem.

NATIONAL MONUMENTS

All national monuments are protected structures and work in their vicinity is strictly controlled. Ideally trails should be kept a <u>minimum of 20m from any national monument</u> and all trail work in the vicinity of these structures should be referred to the National Monuments Service before commencing any work.

FELLING LICENCE

If felling any trees in the course of the trail work, the trail manager or the landowner will need to get a felling licence for any tree more than 15m from a dwelling. Contact the local Forest Service office for details.

14 NATIONAL MONUMENTS are an important part of our heritage that must be protected.

SURVEYING NEW ROUTES

In Chapter 3 we mentioned the old carpenter's adage of 'measure twice and cut once'. Having marked the possible trail corridor on the map, considering the control points, the topography, the ground conditions and likely trail usage, it is now possible to go on site and flag the **outline corridor**.

Following the trail corridor map, flag the trail on the ground. Flagging the corridor allows the trail designer to see the terrain of the proposed trail route and the different conditions that will need to be considered in construction. Walk the trail several times and adjust the route to avoid difficult areas for construction or to take in or avoid positive and negative control points. When you are happy with the route it is now possible to do a detailed survey and specification.

15 FLAGGING TAPE

Surveying a new route will require posts and lump hammer, marker pens, flagging tape, a note book and pencil, a high visibility jacket and a measuring wheel or tape. A Dictaphone is also helpful allowing the trail surveyor to take better notes.

The ideal post for route marking is approximately 50mm X 50mm by about 400mm long (See Figure 16). These can be driven into the ground and marked with adhesive flagging tape and a permanent felt marker to mark the location.

16 EXAMPLE OF A ROUTE MARKING POST

A **high visibility jacket** is very useful when marking in a forest situation where light levels can be lower and way finding difficult. Flagging tape can also be used to mark out the 'early' routes before the final specification is complete with the posts and route notes (See Specification P83).

Hi VISIBILITY JACKETS

MATERIALS
Materials used for trails should be selected on the basis of:
* Durability,
* Availability,
* The cost of the materials and their transportation to the work site,
* Ease of use,
* Appearance,
* And compatibility with the terrain and trail experience

The materials (and methods) used in the construction of a trail should be compatible with the environment in which they are being used. Unsuitable materials will detract from the user's experience and may not be fit for purpose. 'Native' or local materials, such as inorganic soil, rock or timber should be sourced near, but off, the trail, out of sight, where possible. One of the benefits of choosing native materials is that they result in a subtler trail and generally go unnoticed.

WOOD
Trees should be cut to the appropriate length and peeled uphill and out of sight of the trail or prepared at the trail site and all debris removed. (Remember you may need a felling licence).

Considering the long-term maintenance costs associates with using untreated wood, the extra cost of treated timber may be a worthwhile investment. Pressure-treated wood may be suitable if transport is available and the timber not permanently immersed in streams or rivers where toxins can leach into the waters.

ROCK /GRAVEL

Use local rock whenever possible. Rock should be sourced off the trail. Avoid cutting bedrock near the trail, as this can leave a visible scar. When working near old structures like walls and ruins avoid the temptation to use these as a source of ready materials – remember these structures are a valuable cultural artifact of those that worked the land before us. All the rock debris not used in trail construction should be removed out of sight of the trail or used as RipRap (See Chapter 14); holes left by removal of rock should be filled with soil, peat, dead branches, brash and other forest litter to ensure they are not a safety hazard.

EXTRACTING SUB SOIL FOR FILL

Borrow pits are used to source sub soil for fill for the trail tread. These can be near the trail, but keep them out of direct view. Pits should be filled with debris and hidden after use. Where possible gather materials from several locations to reduce feeder trail damage.

BARK MULCH

Occasionally trail builders may be tempted to use bark mulch to construct trails. Except where a trail is required for temporary use – a month or two – bark mulch has no value for trail construction as it absorbs water and quickly breaks down.

TRAIL BUILDER'S HINT

When selecting your route avoid, where possible, areas of deep peat or wet organic soils.

17 MOVING MATERIALS ONTO THE WORK SITE CAN BE COSTLY AND SLOW IN REMOTE OR DIFFICULT AREAS.
A trail builder moving rock with a cable system on the
Appalachian Trail at Bear Mountain, N.Y.

5. TRAIL MAINTENANCE

MAINTENANCE IS CRITICAL

All trails, no matter how well constructed or designed, require maintenance. The actions of feet, tyres, frost, rain, wind and gravity all work over time to damage the trail and therefore require constant maintenance. However, if trails get regular maintenance and attention they will require very little investment in labour or materials for large-scale repair and will remain serviceable for years.

Ideally trails should be inspected and routinely maintained two to three times a year. As with trail construction concentrate on water management and keeping users on the constructed trail; remember the basic rule 'keep water off the trail and users on the trail'.

ADOPT-A-TRAIL

Volunteers are often willing to undertake trail maintenance through adopt-a-trail programmes. Adopt-a-trail volunteers should be required to sign up to maintaining a trail for a minimum of a year.

leave cut log to the side of the trail

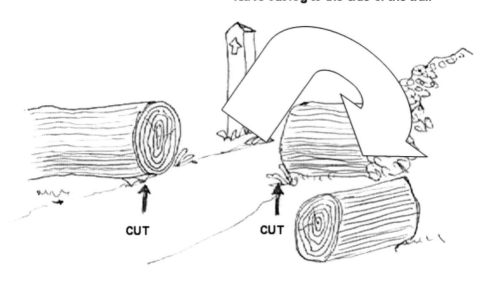

Trail maintainers should inspect the trail a minimum of three times a year.
Early spring, mid summer and early winter are the three important times to inspect and maintain trails.

Early spring will remove any material after winter storms, repair water damage and clean drains and blow-downs.
Mid summer will deal with the impact of usage during the peak season, litter, damage to way-marking, boot leg trails and in particular the heavy growth in vegetation that can sometimes cover way-marking and encroach on trails.
Early winter will make sure the trail is ready for the onslaught of bad weather. Ensure drains are clean and there is no damage to the treadway.

TRAIL ADOPTERS SHOULD LOOK AT:

WATERBARS AND DRAINAGE.
Waterbars, grade dips, side drains and cross drains should be inspected and cleared where required. Vegetation and debris should be cleared from the drain, as this will tend to block water flow, which can lead to wash outs in periods of heavy weather.

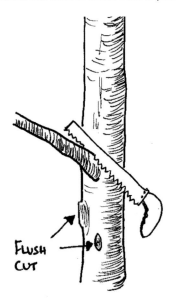

BLOW-DOWNS AND VEGETATION MANAGEMENT.
Trees and vegetation will continue to grow along the trail edge. Ensure that vegetation is cut back from the trail and the trail is fully passable. Blown down trees can also hinder users of the trail and will lead to detours and unwanted new trails. A simple cut to the log in two places to allow for passage is sufficient. Check that trees along the corridor have no potential eye hazards from branches. See Trail Clearance Chapter 15.

WAY-MARKING AND SIGNAGE.
Make sure that all way-marking is clear and visible along the trail and unobstructed by vegetation. Check that all way marks are present and correct and replace markers where required.

STEPS AND TRAIL DEFINERS.
Occasionally trail users may decide to avoid steps and use the ground adjacent to the trail. Use RipRap or brash to deter these bootleg trails.

THE ONE-IN-SEVEN APPROACH
I am interested in volunteering but how much time should I give?
In addition to finding time to hike or cycle, most people have busy lives with jobs, other hobbies and families. Performing trail conservation work can be down the list of things to do despite people's best intentions. In Mountain Meitheal we promote the **one in seven** approach – for every six days you walk or cycle give one day back through trail work.

6. ELEMENTS OF A TRAIL

A trail is a recreation corridor that traverses the countryside giving access to recreational users.

It is important, in both the management and construction of trails, that trail managers and trail crews understand the elements that make up a sustainable trail and their importance in maintaining the trail in a sustainable condition. Different trail elements (Figure 18-A & 18-B) and solutions are often required to deal with changing terrain conditions (Figure 19).

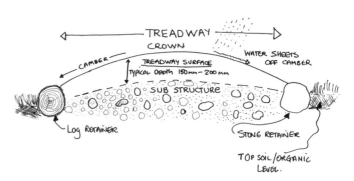

18-A TRAIL ELEMENTS

SUSTAINABLE TRAILS

Sustainability is defined as using a resource today without impacting on the next generation's ability to have the same experience. Sustainable trails should therefore strive to provide a recreation experience without impacting on the environment. Sustainable trails should *sit lightly on the land.*

THE TREADWAY

The treadway is the walking or cycling surface and **must be a durable surface**. Durable surfaces can be compacted crushed stone, rock when used in stone pitched trails, timber trails such as bog bridges or boardwalks, or natural well-drained surfaces such

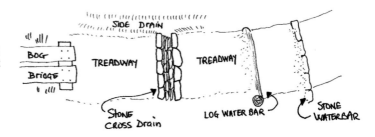

18-B TRAIL ELEMENTS

as rock slabs, compacted sub soils or grass surfaces with thick swards. The treadway width will vary depending on the class and usage of the trail with trails in highly used areas being wider (1500mm – 2500mm) than those in remote areas (800mm – 1000mm). (Figure 18-A).

SUSTAINABLE TRAILS SHOULD HAVE FOUR KEY CRITERIA.

A sustainable trail ......
- Is designed and constructed to minimize erosion and maintenance
- Meets the needs of it's users and provides enjoyable experiences
- Protects the land and the landscape
- Minimizes conflict between different user groups

19 ELEMENTS OF A TRAIL.
On this trail the Mountain Meitheal crew used a turnpike in the foreground and a a bog bridge across the wet area to deal with the different ground conditions.

CROWN

The surface of the treadway should form a **crown** or cambered **convex surface**, which sheds water off to the side of the trail (Figure 18-A.) and thus avoids puddles and water lodging on the trail that eventually leads to potholes and erosion.

METALLED SURFACE

The *metalled* surface is the layer of crushed stone, rock or stone dust (Figure 18-A), which is applied to form the surface of the trail and compacted to provide a durable tread. In more developed parks (such as the core areas of national parks, forest parks or regional municipal parks) the metalled surface will often be of tarmac or similar bonded surfaces (Figure 8 above).

WATERBARS AND GRADE DIPS

The single biggest impact on trails under Irish conditions is water. Water moving along a trail will quickly erode the treadway and ultimately destroy the trail. Waterbars and grade dips (Figure 18-B) are critical for water management particularly in trails with slopes of over 8°.

SIDE DRAINS AND CROSS DRAINS

Side drains and cross drains are an essential element of the water management scheme for all trails. (Figure 18-B.) These should be sufficiently wide to allow for occasional cleaning with a spade or hazel hoe. Water management and the structures used to control water on trails are dealt with fully in Chapter 8.

GRADIENTS

Ideally a trail should not exceed 50% of the side-slope on which it is located (Figure 62). If the trail is more than 50% of the side slope it is called a fall-line trail and should be avoided where possible. Fall line trails involve costly anti erosion measures such as stone steps and a large number of waterbars.

Cycle trails should average not more than 15% gradient and not exceed more than 30% gradient for any section of more than 20m along its length. See Appendix I for trail gradients.

TRAIL BUILDER'S HINT

When building a trail it is essential to remove all the organic material (peat, leaf litter etc.) off the treadway as this material has low load bearing capacity, retains water longer and is more prone to erosion.

SUBSTRUCTURE
This is the main structural element of the trail. It is generally constructed from stone or a stone/gravel mix. Figure 18-A.

RETAINERS
Retainers are used when constructing raised treadway in areas of high water table. They can be constructed from logs, rock or from sawn timber in formal locations such as close to visitor centres or in urban parks.

20 ANCHORS
The big boulders on the right act as anchors as they cause the trail to wrap around and add visual interest to the walker.

ANCHORS
Anchors are used to add interest to a trail and to guide users along the trail. They can include rocks, trees or similar objects, which attract the eye of the user (Figure 20) and serve as a natural anchor for the trail and provide interest to the walker as they move along the trail.

BOG BRIDGES AND BOARDWALKS
are used to cross high water tables or wet peat soils or soils susceptible to damage (e.g. sand dunes).

ROOTS ON A TRAIL
Roots can be an issue when constructing a trail.

- If roots are at 90° to the tread, fairly flush with the surface and not a tripping hazard, leave them in place.

- Remove roots that are parallel with the tread. Parallel roots tend to funnel water along the trail, which causes erosion and also creates a slipping hazard.

- Route your trail above large trees. Building trails below trees undermines their root systems and can eventually kill the trees.

FINALLY, SOME QUESTIONS THAT NEED TO BE ASKED ABOUT TRAIL SUSTAINABILITY IN REMOTE LOCATIONS.

Will the work protect the natural habitat of the trail corridor and it's adjacent lands?
Will the work protect the diversity and character of the trail?
Does the trail work diminish the sense of solitude or take away the challenge to hill walkers' or bikers' skill and stamina?

The answer should be yes to the first two and no to the last question, if not rethink the solutions.

7. SOILS

A basic working understanding of soils is essential when designing or laying out a new trail network. Wet soils have a lower weight bearing capacity than dry soils. (This is evident if you have ever walked across a wet peat bog. In wet weather conditions you will sink, while during a dry period the peat will easily carry you.) Therefore when trail building we need to avoid wet soils or 'soils' that retain water and remain wet for long periods.

If we cut a slice down through the ground we open what is called a soil profile. This profile will expose different layers or horizons.

THE ORGANIC LAYER

Starting from the top we generally have an organic layer of humus, leaf litter or peat (Figure 21). In Ireland where the organic element often forms a deep layer it is known as peat. A layer of organic material can also occur in forests and paths under trees where there is a lot of leaf litter or other vegetation. These organic soils retain water longer and when wet have a lower weight bearing capacity. They are also more prone to erosion as they are lighter than inorganic subsoil and therefore are easily washed away. When dry they are lighter than other soil particles and therefore can be blown more easily. In general the organic layer is unsuitable for trail building.

If used as part of the treadway, the organic layer in time will become waterlogged with traffic and therefore it should always be removed.

SUB SOILS

Below the organic layer we have the sub soil. This is derived from the parent bedrock or from glacial or alluvial deposits. This layer is made up of clay, silt, rocks and boulders and sand.

Unfortunately for us in Ireland much of our upland 'soils' are either peat or are mineral soils with impeded drainage caused by an iron pan. Iron pans are a layer impervious to water formed by ferrous (iron) material being leached down through wet soils (Figures 21 and 22). Sub soils are an excellent source of materials for building reversal trails, see p38.

21 THE SOIL PROFILE with organic soil above the orange trowel and mineral soil below.

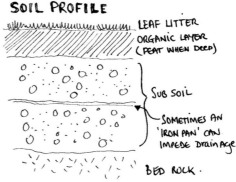

22 A TYPICAL SOIL PROFILE

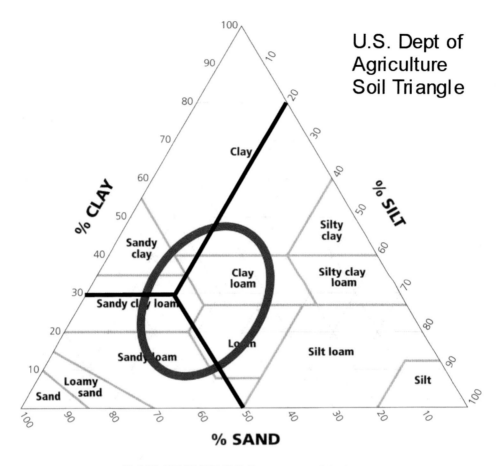

23 SOIL TRIANGLE (U.S. Department of Agriculture)

HOW DO SOILS WORK?

Soils are made up of clay, sand and silt. The percentage of these elements in the inorganic soil layers give them their **carrying capacity**, **drainage qualities** and **ability to bind together**. The clay and silt components of a soil bind the other particles together while sand provides drainage.

Consider walking on sand; while sand trails are well drained and will, if well compacted, support weight, sand does not bind together and therefore tends to be subject to movement and erosion. Walking on a surface with high clay content is often very wet and sticky because the clay element has poor drainage and lower carrying capacity.
Soils with a good balance of clay, silt, sand and gravel give the best trail surfaces. For example a sandy clay loam – made up of **50 percent sand**, **30 percent clay** and **20 percent silt** – will provide a well-drained and bound surface (Figure 23).

REMEMBER ORGANIC MATERIAL – PEAT AND LEAF OR NEEDLE LITTER – HAS ABSOLUTELY NO VALUE AS A MATERIAL FOR USE IN TRAIL BUILDING.

8. WATER AND WATER MANAGEMENT

A simple rule for trail builders is 'keep the users on the trail and the water off'. Running water on any slope that is free of vegetation will cause erosion (Figure 24). The steeper the slope, the faster the water flows (and often the greater the volume as water is coming in from higher ground), with the result erosion occurs if the water flow is unchecked. Therefore, drainage and keeping paths dry, or at least not waterlogged, is a key to path maintenance. (See Trail Definers on how to keep walkers on the trail.)

HOW DO WE KEEP WATER OFF TRAILS?

There are several techniques that can be used to remove water from trails.

These include:
• WATERBARS – ROCK AND LOG
• GRADE REVERSALS OR DIPS
• CULVERTS AND STONE DRAINS

The figures below show different water management techniques.

24 EROSION caused by water on the Wicklow Way. This gully was over 400mm deep. (Photo Shay Walsh)

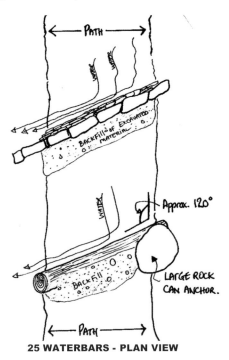

25 WATERBARS - PLAN VIEW

WATERBARS

Waterbars, constructed from either rock or timber, are very effective in slowing down and removing water from a trail.

Cycle or multi-use trails (trails used for wheelchairs, buggies, etc.,) will require dips or grade reversals instead of waterbars.

Waterbars should be set at an angle of approximately **120°** to the main direction of the trail. See Figure 25. An angle **greater than 120°** can result in the water running off too quickly which can cause rutting at the back of the bar. If **less than 120°** the water will not run off effectively and could continue to erode the path. In Figure 25 we see how waterbars should be laid in relation to the general direction of the path.

CONSTRUCTING STONE WATERBARS

First dig a trench and place rocks for the waterbar in the trench to about 2/3 of their depth. Figure 26.

Rocks should typically be set about 300mm deep.

Line the drain bottom with small stones to protect the upper side of the waterbar from rutting - these also help to wedge the waterbar in place.

Use the excavated material to backfill on the lower side of the waterbar.

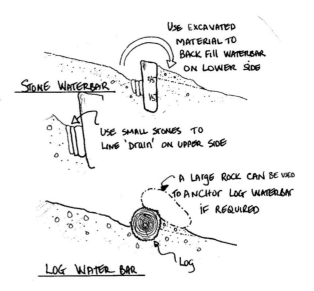

26 CROSS SECTION OF WATERBARS

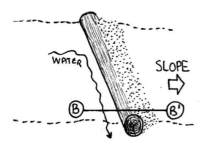

To ensure the full capture of water on the trail make sure that the bar extends slightly beyond the edges of both sides of the trail.

TIMBER WATERBARS

Timber waterbars (Figure 27) are a very effective method of constructing water diversion in areas where stone is limited or where the waterbars are not subject to constant wetting (and therefore rotting). Timber waterbars are cheaper and faster to install.

Typically the log should be approximately **250 – 350mm** in diameter and of a durable timber such as larch. Dig a trench approximately **150 – 200mm** in depth Place the log in the trench and backfill on the lower side with the excavated material. (Figure 27).

Large rocks can be used to anchor the waterbar at one or both ends. Ensure the outfall isn't blocked!

27 LOG WATERBAR

TRAIL BUILDER'S HINT

Walk the trail on a wet day.
Inspecting a trail on a wet day is a great idea – you see where water is coming from AND where water is causing a problem on the trail.

GRADE REVERSALS AND KNICKS

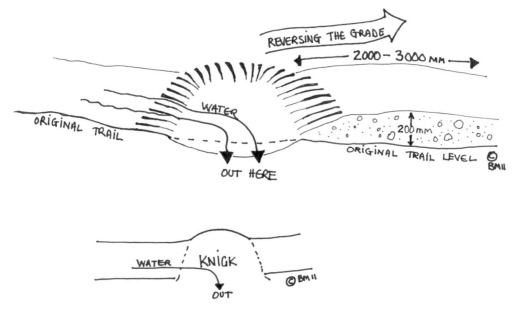

28 GRADE REVERSALS and KNICKS

Where the use of stone or log waterbars is not possible because the trail is a multi-access trail or is a mountain bike trail, which means that waterbars or cross drains would cause an obstruction to passage, then **grade reversals** provide a simple and effective method of taking water off the treadway. Grade reversals are easy and cheap to construct. A grade reversal is simply a shallow trench with a low berm on the downhill side of the trench, See Figure 28. The berm reverses the general gradient of the trail and this causes the water to be shed off the treadway. The berm is constructed by adding approximately 200mm of aggregate to the trail surface over a distance of between 2000 – 3000mm along the trail below the depression.

Modern thinking on water management[2] recommends the use of **KNICKS** as the best and most effective way of removing water. Knicks are simple semi circular depressions on the trail above the berm. Water flows into the knick and sheds off the trail through the open side of the knick. The opening is constructed on the lower side of the trail. Grade reversals and knicks are simple to clean and repair however they there use is limited on trails with gradients above 1-in-5.

CROSS DRAINS

Occasionally there will be a requirement to take water across a trail; possibly connecting side drains on both sides of the trail. This is best achieved using an open stone lined drain. This is a better option than culverts.

WHY NOT USE A CULVERT?

Culverts, unless large diameter pipes are used, can easily become choked with *Molinia* or similar grasses and vegetation. In times of flood this can cause the culvert to block with the result that the drain will fail which can lead to the washout of the trail. An open stone drain (Figure 29) is more effective than culverts in that it tends to self-scour and can be easily cleaned.

---

2 The US Forest Service trail management manual available on line.

When constructing a stone drain ensure that the drain is sufficiently wide enough to allow cleaning with a spade.

Cross drains should have stone walls and a stone floor constructed using smaller stone (See Figure 31). This ensures that water doesn't erode the bottom of the drain.

When using an excavator to construct trails it is possible to use large boulders to construct the edges of the open drains – this is a very effective method and has been used widely on machine-constructed trails by the Forestry Commission in Scotland (Figure 30) and on reversal trails in Ireland.

29 STONE CROSS DRAIN (Photo Shay Walsh)

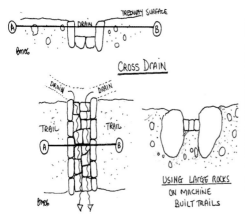

31 STONE CROSS DRAINS

30 OPEN DRAIN CROSSING CONSTRUCTED USING LARGE BOULDERS.

CULVERTS

Culverts are an excellent method of taking water across a trail where fast flowing water is going to present a problem or where obstacles such as waterbars are not acceptable. Ensure the culvert is of **sufficient dimension** to take flash floods that may occur. Always err on the larger side.

CULVERTS CAN BE CONSTRUCTED USING FLAGS AS THE ROOF OVER A STONE DRAIN OR USING CONCRETE PIPES. FIGURES 32/33.

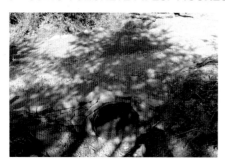

32 CULVERT – Culverts are used where large volumes of water need to be carried under the trail. Note the size of the pipe. The constructed wall to the side and above the pipe protects the trail from erosion.

FABRICATED WATERBARS

At developed sites – on trails close to car parks in forest or national parks – fabricated waterbars (Figure 34) can be used in place of more rustic stone or log solutions. Constructing a box-like structure from treated timber and burying it flush with the surface of the trail is an effective method of installing these types of water management features. Concrete fabricated drainage systems, with a grate cover, are available on the market.

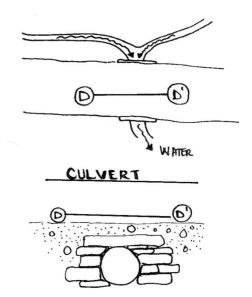

33 CULVERTS – Cross section and plan view.

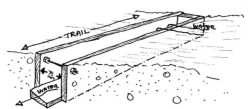

34 FABRICATED TIMBER WATERBAR

TRAIL BUILDER'S HINT

How far apart should waterbars and grade reversals be?

Install a waterbar for every 10 feet of rise along the trail.
So for a 1-in-10 gradient install a waterbar every 100 feet. For a 1-in-5 gradient, install a waterbar every 50 feet.

INSTALL THE FIRST WATERBAR AT THE TOP OF THE TRAIL.

9. TRAIL TYPES

In as much as any trail can be described as a 'standard' trail (Figure 35) the simplest constructed trail is one on **a level, well-drained site**. This is constructed by first removing the leaf litter and humus (the organic) layer. The humus layers retain water, quickly deteriorate into a poor walking or biking surface when wet and have low load bearing properties. The removed material should be scattered <u>well</u> away from the trail to avoid creating any drainage problems on the trail. The tread way is then constructed by using a layer of crushed stone (approximately **200mm** deep) that is finished with a layer of finely crushed stone down to dust[3] to a depth of approximately

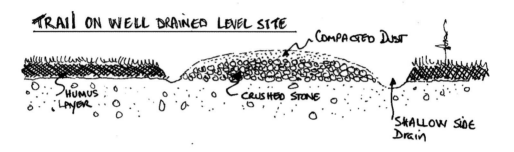

35 'STANDARD' TRAIL CONSTRUCTION ON A LEVEL WELL DRAINED SITE

50mm and compacted with a whacker plate. To ensure good drainage, open a **shallow drain** to the side and create a **cambered** (convex) crown on the trail.

BENCH CUT TRAILS

Bench cut trails are used on cross slopes where the underlying material is sufficiently stable to remain in place even when wet. There are two types of bench cut trails – **full bench cut** (Figure 36) and **half bench cut**.

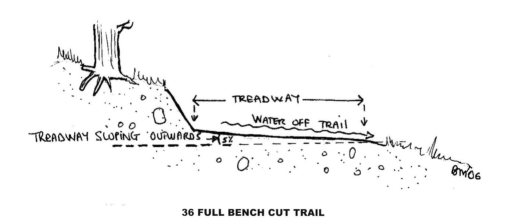

36 FULL BENCH CUT TRAIL

---

3 This is often referred to as 'two inch down' in quarries as it includes stone and dust that will pass through a two-inch screen.

FULL BENCH CUT TRAILS

Full Bench Cut trails are the most stable trail to construct on well-drained and sloping sites. The method of construction is simple – cut into the hillside excavating at least the width of the trail (generally no more than 800mm –1000mm) and deposit all spoil on the lower side of the slope. The slope across the trail treadway should be at approximately 3%-5% out from the hill (Figure 36). This allows water to sheet across the trail. The upper side-wall should be tapered and shaped into the upper slope to avoid collapse onto the trail.

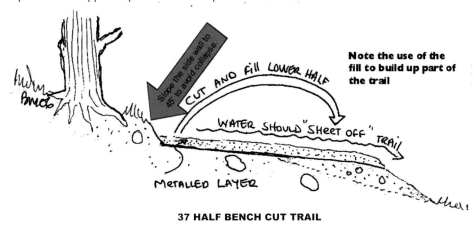

37 HALF BENCH CUT TRAIL

HALF BENCH CUT TRAILS

The half bench cut method is a less stable form of the bench cut trail as it relies on constructing the tread way on the reconstructed lower side. If constructed correctly (i.e. if the material is well compacted) it can be used successfully. Care should be taken when using this method to excavate and dispose of all humus material, particularly under the section that will be built up, before using any of the 'structural' material to construct the treadway. **Where half bench cut trails are constructed on a steep slope it may be necessary to construct a buttress on the lower side to give more stability to the trail.** (See page 59)

Water management! While bench cut trails are used on hillside slopes they will require either waterbars or grade reversals along the trail, otherwise water can still move along the trail and cause erosion.

TURNPIKES

Where the site has a high water table an alternative to bog bridges (See Chapter 10) is to construct a turnpike or raised causeway trail. Essentially a turnpike (Figure 38) raises the walking surface above the water table and thereby minimises water lying on the tread, which will eventually lead to trail erosion.

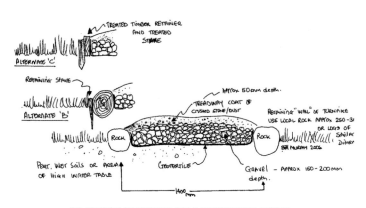

38 CROSS SECTION OF A TURNPIKE TRAIL

Constructing a turnpike is relatively simple. First construct retaining edges for the trail. These can be either rock, the most sustainable; logs in a forest or similar environment or treated sawn timber in more 'formal' landscapes (See Figure 38 above.). If using rock for the retaining boundary use the largest rock possible and dig a small trench for the rocks to sit into (See Figure 39). If using logs or sawn timber it will be necessary to use a retaining stake to hold the timber in place. Once the retaining edges are in place lay a **geotextile** or layer of **brashing** (for example a layer of fresh conifer tree branches) between the retaining edges. This will stop the next layer of rubble/ large stone from being pushed down into the wet layer below. Add the structural layer of rubble/crushed stone or river rocks to a depth of approximately 200mm. Finish with a layer of gravel or crushed stone and compact well. There should be a slight crown on the surface to ensure water runs off both sides

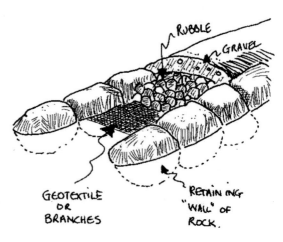

39 CUTAWAY OF A TURNPIKE TRAIL

40 A COMPLETE TURNPIKE TREADWAY using log retainer walls, in-filled with large rock and finished with crushed stone.

Ideally use a local stone – for example in areas with limestone bedrock use crushed limestone or in granite areas use granite sand.

REVERSAL TRAILS
Reversal trails are increasingly being used for the construction of sustainable paths and are a very cost effective method of crossing wet areas.

Reversal trails can be used where there is a covering of peat (a depth of up to 1000mm of peat) and a suitable underlying material such as boulder till or similar material that, when excavated, can provide a suitable substructure.

Reversal paths are constructed using an excavator, ideally a two tonne machine. A small bucket is the best attachment for constructing walking or cycling trails.

CONSTRUCTING A REVERSAL TRAIL
Step 1. (Figure 41). The machine operator clears the peat layer down to the mineral sub soil. The section cleared should be at least twice the width of the path required. The initial cleared area should be approximately 20m^2 (2m wide by about 10m long). The removed peat is piled to the side of the cleared trail corridor and will be used to refill the borrow pits.

41 REVERSAL TRAIL - STEP 1.

Step 2. The machine operator, now sitting on the cleared area, opens a borrow pit working on half the cleared area and excavates the underlying mineral subsoil and piles the mineral subsoil on the final trail line. The subsoil is then shaped to give a camber to allow the trail to shed water (Figure 42).

(The first pile of excavated peat is spread away from the trail.)

Step 3. The operator clears a new section of peat and deposits all the excavated peat, from this section, in the borrow pit of the preceding section. (Figure 43) The operator now excavates a new borrow pit and constructs a new section of elevated trail.

42 REVERSAL TRAIL - STEP 2

43 REVERSAL TRAIL - STEP 3

Step 4. Next (Figure 44) the machine operator tracks along the roughly formed trail to compact and form the camber and install cross drainage or waterbars as required.

Finally the borrow pit is filled with the organic layer (often peat) and the spoil is leveled and landscaped.

Further manual work may be required to add waterbars, complete landscaping. Planting or grass seeding maybe necessary to aid the re-vegetation of the adjacent land.

Some reversal trails will require a metalled surface to complete their construction. Where this is necessary the treadway should be finished with approximately 100mm of 50mm stone with dust binding.

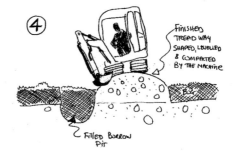

44 REVERSAL TRAIL - STEP 4

STONE PITCHED TRAILS AND STONE 'STAIRCASES'

Stone pitched trails are the most expensive trails to construct in terms of manpower and materials (if these have to be imported onto the site). However, where used they provide the most durable and sustainable trail solution.

Choice of rock is essential. The rock for stone pitching will ideally have a <u>flat top surface</u> and a <u>cone shaped lower part</u> that will anchor the trail into the ground. Use rocks that are shaped like molar teeth, the teeth that grind, see Figure 46. Rocks for stone pitching should ideally be the size of a football or bigger. Large rocks already in situ can be used to anchor the trail using smaller rocks as infill, to create the treadway.

**45 COMPLETED REVERSAL TRAIL -
note the landscaped edges to the trail
and the stone waterbar in the
foreground.**

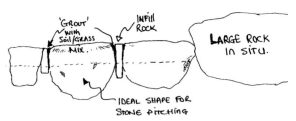

46 ROCK TYPE FOR STONE PITCHING

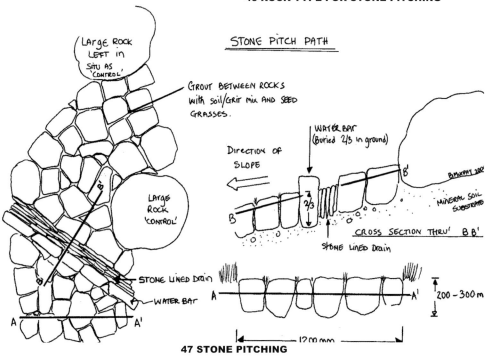

47 STONE PITCHING

It is essential to use rock local to the area – granite in a granite area, old red sandstone in an ORS area – for both aesthetic reasons and compatibility with the local geology.

The Cross Section BB (Figure 47) shows the arrangement for dealing with waterbars as part of a stone pitched route. The waterbars may need to be connected to **collector drains** above and below the stone pitched section to cut off the flow of water onto the trail.

48 STONE PITCHED TRAIL - Torc Mountain Path, Killarney National Park, using imported rock.

GROUTING

Stone pitched trails should ideally be finished by brushing in a mix of soil and grass seed as a grout between the stone. This will give the trail a more mature finish and also help to bind the trail surface together and stop erosion.

The picture of the stone pitched trail in Killarney (Figure 48) shows the value of grouting with grass seed and soil mix. Although this photograph was taken less than two months after completion of the work the grass gives it a more mature and natural look and feel. (These rocks are green sandstone – indigenous to the park – and while they look flat they are in fact up to 350mm deep.)

49 STONE STAIRCASE
This trail was built with local material arranged in such a way as to form a very durable walking surface. (Curtlestown Forest, Glencree, Co. Wicklow)

LOCAL ROCK

The stone staircase on the Wicklow Way was built entirely from rock sourced locally ensuring no change in soil pH (acidity) because of the importation of non-local rock. It also created a trail that blended with the surroundings

HOW MUCH ROCK PER METER OF TRAIL?

Assuming a trail with an approximate width of 1200mm, you will require in the region of one tonne of rock per linear meter.

10. BOG BRIDGES AND BOARD WALKS

Ireland has many boggy areas where trail construction can present real difficulties in terms of finding a sustainable solution that is cost effective and does not impact too heavily on the landscape. Peat, especially when wet, has very low ground bearing capacity and is a very poor walking surface for any trail. Continued trampling of the vegetation on peat often results in a quagmire after the loss of the vegetation. Once the heather or grass on bog is destroyed the erosion of the peat layers will be accelerated. Peat when exposed and dry is very prone to wind erosion and subsequently, rutting. Similarly sand dunes and salt marshes have very fragile soils where erosion can be a problem and where heavily engineered aggregate or stone trails such as turnpikes (See Chapter 9) may not be the right solution.

How do we cross these wet or fragile areas? There are a number of ways and these include **boardwalks**, **bog bridges**, and **eco grid**.

BOG BRIDGES AND BOARDWALKS

The simplest form of trail construction in this case is the rustic Bog Bridge, used to cross short stretches of wet ground. Rustic bog bridges can be constructed from split logs (use larch or other durable timber) nailed to cross pieces (See rustic bog bridge below). These are ideal as temporary solutions to short sections of wet trail.

For more durability it will be necessary to construct bog bridges from treated timber. You need to consider the use of treated timber carefully as this may be incompatible with nature conservation objectives if used in Special Areas of Conservation.

50 BOG BRIDGE TRAIL.
This trail crosses a wet area of peat on a mountain access route in the Dublin Mountains.

Figures 51/52 show a typical bog bridge construction using timber the same dimensions as old railway sleepers. As can be seen from the diagram, construction is simple. Bull wire or similar straps are used to fix the lengths to the crossties. It is also essential to **ensure the 'sleepers' have a good grip underfoot** as they can get

Nails

"RUSTIC" BOG BRIDGE

extremely slippery when wet. Wire netting is sometimes used to give grip to sleeper bogbridges although the wire can get clogged with mud and wet peat. A better solution is to use wire staples and leave the staples slightly proud of the wood to provide the grip.

SAFETY NOTE!! SLEEPERS ARE EXTREMELY HEAVY – ALWAYS ENSURE THERE ARE SUFFICIENT HANDS TO MOVE THEM INTO PLACE.

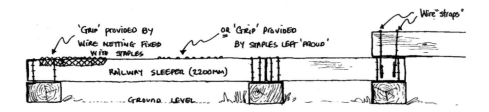

51 SLEEPER BOG BRIDGE – Side View.

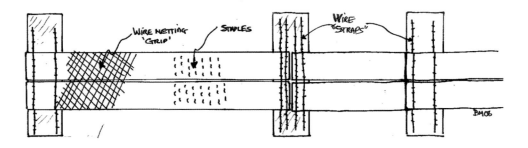

52 SLEEPER BOG BRIDGE - Plan View.

HOW MANY SLEEPERS DO YOU NEED?

Railway sleepers are approximately 2200 mm in length. Two full sleepers are required to cross 2200 mm. To construct a bog bridge you will also need two cross pieces of approximately 1100mm at each end as stringers.

To construct 11 meters of boardwalk you will require:

5 X 2 full sleepers + 6 X half sleepers (for the cross pieces)
= 5 X 2 + 6 X .5 = 13 sleepers
+ One extra sleeper to allow for occasional steps.

Therefore 1 meter of boardwalk will require 14/11 or approximately 1.25 sleepers.

While railway sleepers give a very durable and strong treadway their use is no longer acceptable because of environmental reasons – leaching of creosote. Treated timber 'sleepers' (rough sawn timber with a typical dimension 100mm X 200mm – 4" X 8") can be used as a more eco-friendly alternative to old railway sleepers and will avoid the use of materials with high creosote content.

53 LIGHT BOG BRIDGE CROSSING A SENSITIVE CONSERVATION SITE.
Note how the trail weaves across the landscape and avoids going in straight lines.
(Glanteenassig, Co. Kerry).

When constructing a bog bridge trail on sloping or uneven ground it may be necessary to use **cross-pieces** to deal with the big differences in ground level. (Figure 54 - top). Using this approach it should be possible to give sufficient support to the trail while traversing uneven terrain.

For more even terrain such as blanket bog or salt marsh the standard method (i.e. using large dimension timber as the cross pieces or sill) can be used (Figure 54 - bottom).

54 SUPPORTS FOR BOG BRIDGES ON SLOPING GROUND

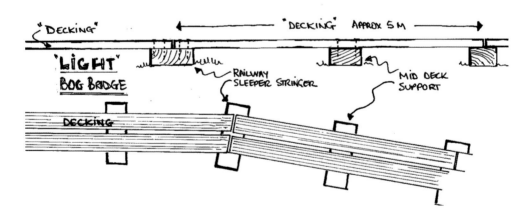

55 LIGHT BOG BRIDGE CONSTRUCTION.
For temporary use or for areas of low usage it is possible to use decking timbers instead of larger dimension timbers. It will, however, be necessary to use more mid deck supports.

BOARDWALKS

While bog bridges are an effective method for crossing sensitive or wet areas for traditional hiking or walking routes they are not suitable for **all ability trails** or for general use in high use areas. All ability trails on sensitive sites (Figure 56) require the construction of boardwalks. Boardwalk trails are also used on sections of mountain bike trails to add interest and to cross wet areas. (Figure 57)

56 MULTI ACCESS BOARD WALK allows easy access to a sensitive sand dune complex in Ards Forest Park, Co. Donegal. (Photo. M. Ruane, Coillte.)

57 BOARD WALK TRAIL Ballyhoura mountain bike trail, County Limerick. (Photo. D. de Forge, Coillte)

Boardwalks should be constructed from treated timber and where possible ground disturbance should be avoided as much as possible. Ideally the boardwalk should be **no more than 200mm** above the surrounding ground. Figure 58 below shows a typical boardwalk construction. The construction method involves posts driven into the ground with **cross stringers** used to support the **longitudinal stringers.** Decking is then fitted to the longitudinal stringers and a toe rail fitted to the edge. Where ground disturbance should be avoided or where the terrain is too soft to hold a post, it is possible to use sleepers as an alternative to the posts and cross stringers.

The longitudinal stringers are then fixed to the half sleepers that act as cross stringers. A **toe rail** should be fitted to the edge to guide wheel chair and buggy users. This is preferable to handrails as these can cause a hindrance to wheel chair users.

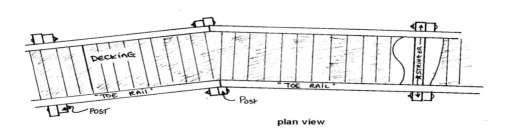

plan view

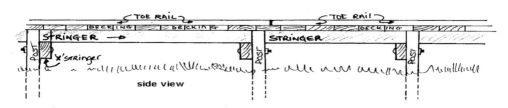

side view

58 BOARD WALK – TYPICAL LAYOUT.

11. MOUNTAIN BIKING TRAILS

Mountain biking is one of Ireland's fastest growing outdoor pursuits and one where trails are needed more than any other outdoor pursuit to ensure sustainability. Good mountain bike trails have exactly the same characteristics as hiking or other recreation trails in that they guide the user through the countryside, provide a challenging and authentic outdoor experience and should be durable and sustainable.

The characteristics that make a hiking trail durable and sustainable are equally applicable to a mountain bike trail – the treadway should be a non-organic surface and water should be kept of the trail.

This chapter deals specifically with issues relating to mountain bike trails however, the construction techniques described in other chapters in the book have as much application to mountain bike trails as to any other form of recreation trail with the exception of features such as waterbars and steps. Mountain bike trail builders would do well to study the general techniques for building bench cut trails, raised treadways and board walks as well as buttresses, water management and the use of trail definers.

59. BENCH CUT CROSS COUNTRY TRAIL.
Note the trail slopes outwards to the right to shed water off the trail. Note also the use of the logs and rock to act as trail definers.

INAPPROPRIATE TRAILS

60 INAPPROPRIATE TRAILS
These trail structures are poorly constructed and dangerous to less skilled users. The trail 'treadway' to the left of the picture is peat and shows signs of erosion.

The issue for many land owners and managers with unauthorised trail building on their land is that the trails are often constructed incorrectly resulting in trails that:

- Are **dangerous** to other less skilled riders,
- Often **cause trail erosion** and therefore are unsustainable,
- Can often **cause damage** to important habitats, cultural features and conservation sites.

PERMISSIONS

It is important before constructing any trails that you have full permission from the land owners and that you also deal with the appropriate permissions regarding **notifiable actions**[4] in SPECIAL AREAS of CONSERVATION, felling licences and working close to national monuments. Failure in this area could result in prosecution and fines. **(See Chapter 4 – Getting Started)**

TRAIL LAYOUTS

Mountain biking trails can be either cross-country or down hill and can be described as either flowing or technical trails. These different trail types will change the design and techniques used in constructing the trail.

As with hiking trails, the trails network should be designed on a stacked loop system with more difficult trails at the furthest point from the trailhead and easier loops close to the trail access point. (This ensures that novice riders do not 'stumble' on to technically difficult trails.)

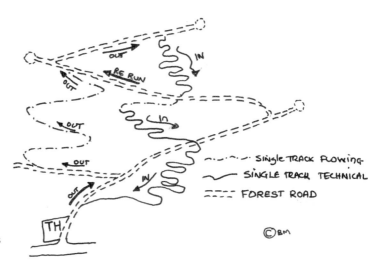

61 TYPICAL MOUNTAIN BIKE TRAIL LAYOUT

Most mountain bike trail layouts in Ireland will make use of existing trails and road infrastructure to develop a full trail network. **Forest roads make good climbing trails but MUST be avoided at all costs for use as descending trails.** Forest roads allow cyclists to build up too much speed on descent and this creates a real hazard of collision when the road is shared with other users – timber trucks, forestry vehicles and walkers. Figure 61 shows a typical trail layout using an existing forest road network. Leaving the Trail Head (TH) the network uses the forest road to climb on the outward loop. A section of flowing trail then allows for an easy climb to the upper road where a road section brings the cyclist to the highest point. Now a section of technical trail provides an interesting but controlled descent. (At this point the rider can return to the highest point using the road.) From the forest road junction the trail uses both flowing trail (across slope) and then technical trail for the final inward descent to the trailhead.

GRADIENTS

Gradients are the key to building durable mountain bike trails. **IMBA**, the International Mountain Bike Association, recommend that the **gradient on a cross-country trail should be less than half the gradient on the cross slope they traverse.** So for example on the cross country trail in Figure 62 the gradient of the trail should be less than 50% of $X°$ where $X°$ is the gradient of the cross slope of the hill.

---

[4] Under EU Directives covering habitats, work that will break ground – drainage work and other trail work – will require permission from the NPWS. You are required to **notify** the NPWS.

This slope maintains an interesting but challenging descent while accommodating good water management, which reduces erosion. Gradients on trails of **over 8° are prone to trail damage** as riders tend to use their brakes to slow down and this results in trail rip.

CROSS COUNTRY TRAILS

Cross-country trails make up the lions share of any mountain bike trail network. They provide the long rides for most riders and are the **most durable** mountain bike trails. The International Mountain Bike Association recommends cross-country trails as the most appropriate trail type to build for general use.

Bench cut trails can generally be used to construct cross-country trails and water management is easily achieved by using **dips** or **grade reversals**. (See Water Management, Chapter 8).

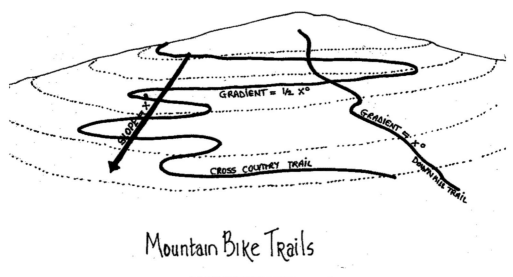

Mountain Bike Trails

62 MOUNTAIN BIKE TRAILS

DOWNHILL TRAILS

Down hill trails are trails that cross the contour lines at a right angle and generally have a slope **equal to that of the slope of the hill**.

Down hill trails are very difficult to construct in such a way as to limit erosion, because it is not generally possible to make full use of dips or grade reversals to manage water. Down hill trails are generally used for competition and are usually temporary in nature. Where a permanent down

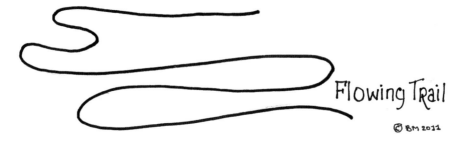

Flowing Trail

© BM 2011

63 FLOWING TRAILS

hill trail is constructed it will generally require a considerable amount of rock armouring to limit trail erosion from water and tyre rip.

FLOWING TRAILS

Cross-country mountain bike trails can be described as **flowing** (Figure 63) or **tight / technical** trails (Figure 64). Flowing trails give a long gentle ride and are more appropriate to trails for less experienced riders or can be used between very technical sections to allow riders to relax. Turns are wide on flowing trails with plenty of opportunity for the rider to see a considerable distance ahead, along the trail. Flowing trails allow cyclists to build up reasonable speeds on descent (See controlling speed below.)

TECHNICAL TRAILS

Trail designers can use technical sections of trails to provide an interesting challenging ride, but it also allows the control of speed.

Technical trails make maximum use of tight turns, switchbacks and grade reversals all of which add to the challenge but will slow down the rate of descent. Using technical trails also allows the trail builder to install a long section of trail in a relatively small area of land and can be useful for urban parks or areas close to cities.

64 TECHNICAL TRAILS

WATER MANAGEMENT ON BIKE TRAILS

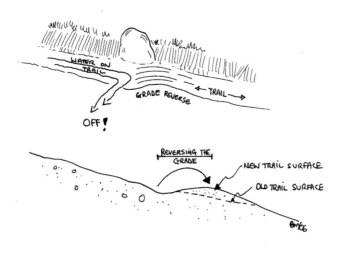

65 GRADE REVERSALS OR DIPS

Water management along MTB trails require solutions other than the use of rock and log waterbars – which are obviously not suitable for bike trails.

Grade reversals or **dips** are the preferred method of getting water off the trail along with constructing trails with a good **side slope** or crown to allow the water to sheet off the trail where possible.

Grade reversals are easy to construct and simply involve building a long and low 'bump' on the trail below a drainage depression that takes the water off the trail (See Figure 65.)

As with waterbars, the depression on the upper side should be at a **120° angle** (approximately) to the direction of the trail to allow water to flow off the trail but not at too much of an angle that would cause erosion.

TREADWAY CONSTRUCTION

Mountain bike trails are no different from other trails in that they must have a constructed treadway capable of carrying continuous traffic. **All organic matter must be removed from the trail** – only inorganic material will provide a suitable trail surface. Ensure that the treadway is constructed to shed water as often as possible by tilting the trail outwards at about 5% (Figure 66) and by using grade reversals.

Bench cut trails are the most widely used method of construction for mountain bike trails in Ireland along with boardwalk trails across very wet areas. Bench cut trails are ideal for water management. Bench cut trails should be constructed along their length at a gradient of less than 50% of the slope across the trail. (See Gradients, Figure 62 above and Appendix I). Bench cut trails should be sloped outwards (from the uphill side) with a 5% slope approximately to carry water off the trail. The lower side of the trail should be cleared of all material – to about 1000mm below the trail – that could obstruct water from sheeting off the trail. During maintenance remove any berm that might develop along the edge of the trail.

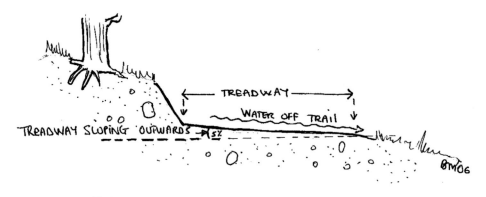

66 BENCH CUT TRAIL
Note the out slope that allows water to sheet off the trail

TRAIL CLEARANCE

When creating a trail corridor for mountain bike use, it is essential to ensure correct **trail clearance.**
Tree branches can be a potentially serious hazard to trail users particularly when travelling at speed. The minimum width of a trail corridor should be **2400mm** to avoid the possibility of contact with branches. Branches should be removed to a height of **2400mm** and **cut flush** with the stem ensuring no stubs are left, which could present a safety hazard, particularly for eyes. **(See Trail Clearance, Chapter 15).**

67 TRAIL CLEARANCES

SIGHT LINE ZONES

As mountain bikes travel at speed, it is essential that riders are aware of what is around the next corner. One of the most important issues to consider in laying out a cycle trail, particularly in a forest, is to ensure **good sight lines** (Figure 68.) Branches should be removed from the bottom two meters of the stem of the tree to allow clear sight lines through the forest.

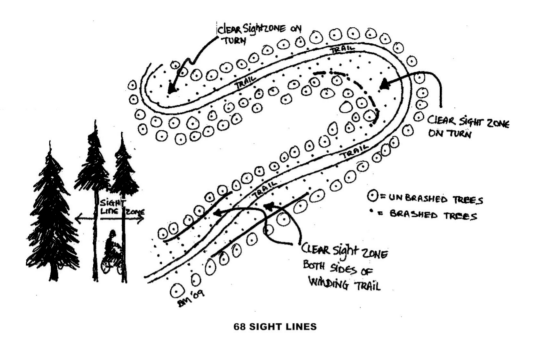

68 SIGHT LINES

Sight line zones should be cleared in the **concave part of any turns** – this allows the rider to see what is around the corner – and up to two meters from the centre of the treadway on winding trails.

69 A MOUNTAIN BIKE TRAIL WITH GOOD SIGHT LINES.
Note the way the trees are pruned (branches removed) up to about 2500mm so that riders can see through the forest and the trail ahead.

CONTROLLING SPEED

As a trail designer, unless you are designing a down hill trail, you will need to control speed. Why? If speed is not controlled riders will tend to use their brakes too often with the result they will skid and cause trail rip. Good trail design will ensure that the rider has an exciting authentic experience, suited to his or her ability, and will not have the perception that their speed is being controlled. How do we do this?

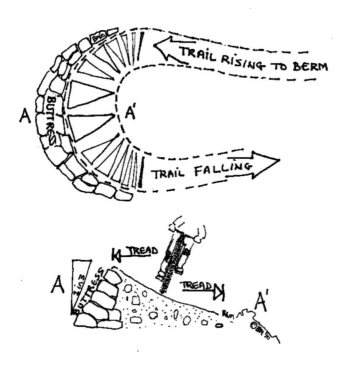

70 BERMS AND SPEED CONTROL
By raising the trail to a berm, the trail designer can control the speed into the turn. Note the 1 in 3 batter on the buttress.

Firstly, if you incorporate forest or other non-public roads into the trail network ensure you take the trail **up hill on these roads** – never down. Permitting cyclists to come down hill on these roads allows for too much speed and increases the chance of accidents with other road users such as walkers and forest vehicles.

For the down hill sections use plenty of tight technical trail – this will ensure an exciting, challenging but slower ride.

Use grade reversals to slow bikes down at key points such as approaching turns or bends. After a nice free flowing descent reverse the gradient so that the bike slows down naturally. Use grade reversals approaching berms – 30m or 50m from the berms, change the slope to an uphill grade and the cyclist will slow down before the turn.

HINTS FOR MOUNTAIN BIKE TRAIL BUILDERS

- Trail gradients should be less than 50% of the cross slope of the trail
- Grade reversals are the best form of water management
- Construct bench cut trails with a 5° out slope
- Ensure good sight lines
- Use grade reversals to control speed
- Technical trails give a slower but challenging ride.

12. BRIDGES

Timber bridges are the most suitable for use on most recreation trails. They can be constructed from either treated sawn timber or alternatively, for a more rustic feel, from round wood. Recycled electricity or telegraph poles make excellent bridge supports and are relatively easy to come by.

TRAIL LAYOUT AND BRIDGE DESIGN

Mountain streams and rivers are often subject to flash flooding which can raise the water level significantly and carry many cubic metres of water at great speed and force. As crossing mountain streams in spate can be hazardous most hiking trails in Ireland require bridges. This is an important consideration in trail network design and bridge locations will be one of the trail control points. It is

71 A FOOT BRIDGE CONSTRUCTED BY MOUNTAIN MEITHEAL VOLUNTEERS IN THE WICKLOW MOUNTAINS.
The bridge is built from old transmission poles and recycled railway sleepers.

essential to take account of these periodic rises and to design the bridge high enough to contend with most floods.

BUTTRESSES AND PLINTHS

To build a bridge capable of dealing with periodic floods it may be necessary to construct a buttress to raise the bridge higher than the existing bank. These can be constructed either using a rock buttress or a log or timber buttress. (See Figure 72 and Chapter 13 below). When constructing log or timber buttresses it is essential to anchor the buttress and the bridge superstructure by burying a ground anchor under the rock or in the ground.

72 RECYCLED RAILWAY SLEEPERS BEING USED FOR THE CONSTRUCTION OF A BRIDGE BUTTRESS.

The foundation of all bridge superstructures is a solid and durable plinth or sill. This should be constructed of durable timber, concrete or rock. The plinth or sill allows the stringer to be kept off the ground and thus not in constant contact with wet soil where it would be more prone to rotting.

Treated sawn timber for the stringers should be a minimum 4"X10" (See Table 5 below for dimensions for differing spans). Alternatively recycled transmission poles give long lengths and a durable pole for bridge construction. The span diameter table provides recommended minimum diameters for various bridge spans (based on a two-stringer bridge). The deck of the bridge can be finished with commercial grade patio decking or similar. Figure 73 gives a typical layout and details for handrails etc. Round timber such as telegraph poles or durable timber such as peeled larch give a more rustic feel. Rustic bridges can be finished with decking and handrails made from pencil posts. As with other timber structures it will be essential to improve the grip and this can be achieved using either chicken wire or wire staples left proud of the decking.

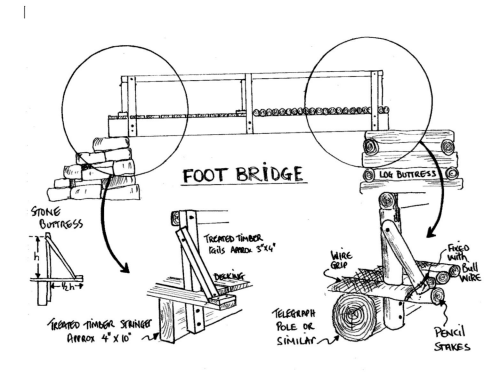

73 STANDARD BRIDGE DESIGN FOR WALKING TRAILS

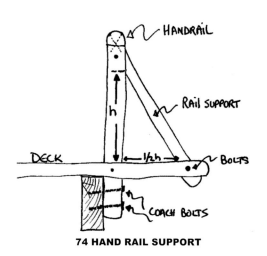

74 HAND RAIL SUPPORT

HAND RAILS

Bracing against the decking as shown in Figure 74 will support the handrail. The bracing should come out at least half the length of the height of the handrail.

SMALL DRAIN CROSSINGS

For drain crossings or small streams a simple bridge constructed in a manner similar to that used for bog bridges is sufficient. (**Figure 75.**) This involves the use of sleepers or similar dimension lumber with a sill or plinth set into the bank.

As with the bog bridges, **improving the grip is essential**. Wire staples left proud can be used to improve grip.

In more primitive recreation areas or areas of low use, logs or trees can also be used to create simple bridges (Figures 75/76). The surface can be shaped with a chainsaw and an adze to give a suitable walking surface. Again, as with the bog bridges, **improving the grip is essential**.

75 A SIMPLE BRIDGE

76 A SIMPLE LOG BRIDGE CROSSING A DRY STREAM.
This log bridge was used on a trail in Muir Woods National Monument, California, to connect two well-used trails.

TABLE 5 DIAMETER DIMENSIONS FOR BRIDGE CONSTRUCTION

* Source: British Columbia Forest Service Recreation Handbook – Recreation Trail Manual

Clear Span (metres)	Douglas-fir Timber (cm) Width x Depth	Peeled Logs mid point Diameter (cm)		
		Fir	Spruce	Cedar
0 - 4.5	15.5 x 20.5	22	24	26
4.8 - 6	20.5 x 26	27	29	31
6.3 - 7.5	20.5 x 31	31	34	36
7.8 - 9	31 x 31	36	38	41
9.3 - 10.5	31 x 36	40	43	46
10.8 - 12	36 x 41	43	49	51
12.3 - 13.5	41 x 41	47	52	56
13.8 - 15	41 x 46	51	57	61

SAFETY!
Bridges and similar constructions should be checked by an engineer before opening for general use and afterwards on a regular basis, particularly after storms.

13. Steps, Crib Walls and Check Dams

STEPS

Steps are often required on upland trails or where the gradient and topography changes quickly. While they can be constructed using timber or stone, stone steps are much more durable and give a longer, more natural looking and relatively maintenance free, solution. There are two typical methods of rock step construction – **over lap** and back fill method.

As with stone pitched paths, the larger the rocks used the more trouble free the path you build. (Moving a large rock may take some time but when in place they will cover a larger area, be more stable and will be well worth the effort.)

STEP DIMENSIONS

The depth of the riser and length of the tread will vary depending on the steepness of the trail.

On a **steep gradient step**, (1-in-2.5 or 22°), a riser of approximately **200mm** and a tread of approximately **500mm** should be used.

On a **moderate gradient,** (1-in-3 or 20°), steps require a **750mm tread** for a **200mm** riser.

To construct a **shallow stairway,** (1-in-4 or 15°), use a tread of approximately 1125mm with a riser of 200mm.

77 STONE STEPS
These provide a 'natural'
and very durable trail solution. Fairy
Castle Trail – Dublin Mountains.

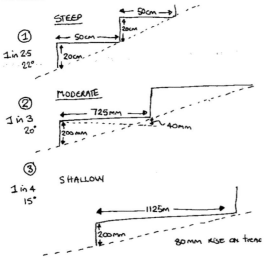

78 DIMENSIONS FOR STEPS

It is essential to slope the steps forwards to allow water to sheet off when constructing earth filled trails. For moderate steps use a 40mm rise from the back to the front of the step. For a shallow step use a difference of approximately 80mm between front and back of the step. See Figure 78.

OVER LAP STONE STEPS

To build stone steps, **START FROM THE BOTTOM** to ensure a good foundation. Clear a foundation for the first rock, allowing for a gentle slope into the hill (Figure 79). This will anchor the step as the rock is lying into the hill and will not tilt outwards when a hiker steps on the edge. Now add the second step above and so on. Allow a riser on the step of approximately 200 – 300 mm (8 inches to one foot) and allow a sufficient depth on the tread to allow the **full foot to fall on the rock** during descent.

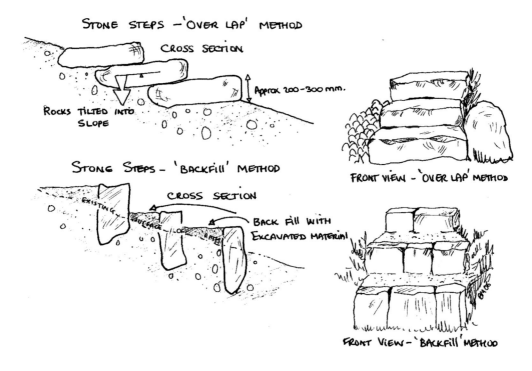

79 STONE STEPS

BACKFILL METHOD
In a similar fashion to constructing a stone waterbar (See construction of waterbars in Water Management, Chapter 8) dig a trench to allow approximately 50-60 % of the rock to be buried. Retain the excavated material and backfill to create a tread way with a slight fall out from the step to shed water (See Figure 79).

REMEMBER THE LARGER THE ROCK USED THE MORE EFFECTIVE THE SOLUTION. ALWAYS START WITH A GOOD FOUNDATION AND BUILD YOUR STEPS UPWARDS.

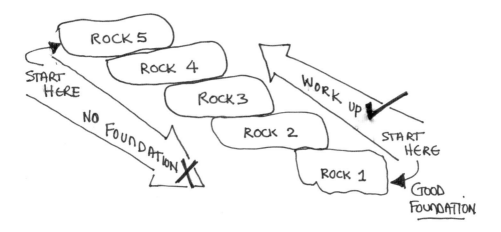

LOG STEPS

Log steps can be used on some trails. Logs should be peeled to reduce rot and chicken wire or staples fixed to their upper surface to give the log grip when wet. Use heavy rocks or posts to hold the logs in place.

Logs can also be dug into the side of the trail when constructing log steps in a gully.

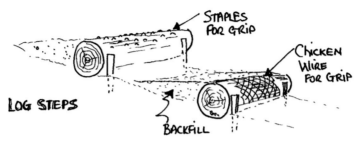

80 SIMPLE LOG STEPS

TREATED TIMBER STEPS

On trails in more developed locations (with a high level of usage), treated timber steps can be an excellent alternative solution to stone or log steps. See Figures 81/82. Fix the timber risers (treated rough sawn timber approximately 70mm X 210mm – 3"X9") to the original ground level, fill with soil or crushed stone and compact with a whacker plate. Ensure a slight out fall to shed water.

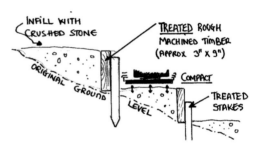

81 TREATED TIMBER STEPS

PRE-FABRICATED STAIRS FOR ROCKY LOCATIONS

Alternatively where fixing individual risers to rocky ground might be too difficult, a stair-type structure can be constructed of trail, moved into place and back filled to create the steps. (Figure 82).

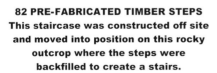

82 PRE-FABRICATED TIMBER STEPS
This staircase was constructed off site and moved into position on this rocky outcrop where the steps were backfilled to create a stairs.

(Kaaterskill Falls State Park, N.Y.)

BUTTRESS AND CRIB WALLS

Buttress, or crib walls (See Figure 83/84/85) may have to be constructed on some side slopes where excavation of a bench cut trail is not possible. Buttress walls are often used at switchbacks or on berms (on mountain bike trails) where the trail may have to be supported on the turns (See Figure 86).

SLOPE THE BUTTRESS INTO THE HILLSIDE.

When constructing a buttress wall, ensure that the rock or logs used in the wall or cribbing are tilted slightly backwards into the slope.
This is the 'batter' of the wall and it should be between 1-in-2 and 1-in-3 to give the greatest stability and anchorage to the buttress on the slope.

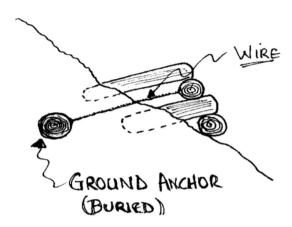

83 BUTTRESS WALLS anchored with ground anchor

Excavate down to a solid foundation before building upwards. <u>Remember to remove all organic material to get to the sub soil or bed rock.</u> Use the largest rock possible on the base to construct a good foundation and to give the wall greater stability. Use large rocks at right angles to the line of the wall to tie the wall to the slope.

Where logs are used to construct a buttress wall it maybe necessary to use ground anchors to tie the buttress into the slope.

84 BUTTRESS WALL constructed from sawn timber and filled with rock rubble on a gully side slope. (Muir Woods Nat. Monument, California, USA.)

85 AN EXCELLENT EXAMPLE OF A BUTTRESS WALL SUPPORTING A TRAIL. (LEFT)
Note the batter of the wall - it slopes back into the trail giving the wall greater stability. Note also the occasional rocks protruding above the top of the wall. These act as definers keeping users back from the edge of the trail.

INSTALLING A GROUND ANCHOR

To install a ground anchor first bury a log in the slope (See Figure 83). This ground anchor log is then tied to one of the buttress logs with a wire strop. The other logs in the construction are tied in turn with strong wire or similar fixing to ensure they are all connected. This ensures that the entire structure is fixed to the slope. Once the frame or wall is complete fill the cribbing with rock rubble of sufficient size to allow for drainage.

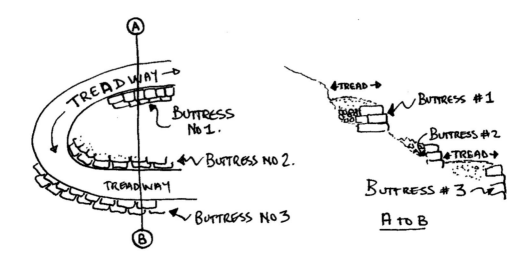

86 BUTTRESS WALLS ON A SWITCH BACK.
Wall # 1 is used to support the tread above the turn.
Wall # 2 is used to stop material falling onto the trail below and wall # 3 supports the tread after the turn.

Hint - Choosing the Right Rock for Buttress Walls

In reality, it is necessary to use the rock that is available on site. However the bigger the rock used the better the result. Long rocks are useful for tying the wall into the slope – when placed at right angles to the wall.

The key to wall building is the foundation and the 'batter'. Establish a solid foundation with the biggest rocks and then slope (batter) the wall slightly off vertical into the slope. Remember to keep some large rocks for the capstones – small rocks can be easily dislodged.

It is possible to split rock with feathers and wedges but this requires that bore holes are drilled first to take these.

CHECK DAMS

Where erosion is advanced (Figure 87) and deep gullies have developed it may be necessary, having established a new trail tread away from the old trail, to aid the restoration of the old trail with the use of check dams.

Check dams (Figure 88) are easily constructed by placing large boulders or logs in the gully to form a dam. Check dams slow or stop moving water, which then deposits silt, stones and seeds. This material will build up behind the dam and eventually re-vegetation will occur.

Steps as Check Dams

Steps can also act as check dams if constructed in a gully or an already badly eroded trail.

Logs are the best method for constructing these steps. The logs should be dug into the side of the gully to provide anchorage. The steps will slow down and stop both water and soil movement while also providing a sustainable tread.

87 This section of trail was so badly eroded it was necessary to establish a new trail corridor. The abandoned trail is suitable for re-vegetation using check dams.

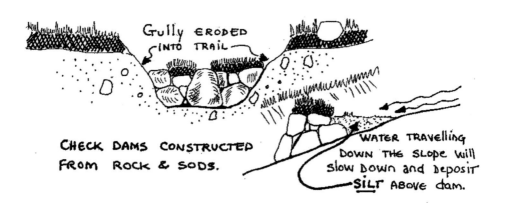

88 CHECK DAMS

14. TRAIL DEFINERS

Occasionally it may be necessary to keep trail users off sensitive sites. **Ideally avoid fences or a lot of signage** both of which can be expensive and also intrusive on the landscape. Several alternate methods can be used to define a trail in a more gentle fashion.

BRASH

Brash is a simple way of persuading users to remain on the trail while protecting the vegetation along the trail edges. It can be also used to block off old or unofficial trails. 'Brashing' simply involves the use of forest branches piled along side the trail and at strategic points where walkers need to be curtailed. (Figure 89).

SCREE WALLS

Scree walls are a very effective method of keeping users off sensitive sites and on the trail.

Scree walls are generally about 150mm – 300mm in height and are constructed from loose stone that is collected from the treadway and adjacent to the trail. This is used to construct a loose wall to each side of the trail which limits trail spread. See **Figures 90.**

89 BRASH used to keep walkers on the steps and off a re-vegetation zone. (Photo Shay Walsh)

Avoid making the walls too regular or straight. Go with the general 'flow' of the path and don't over build the wall or get into fancy stonework – they should nearly be invisible. Regular maintenance once or twice a year may be required to repair and maintain these loose stone walls.

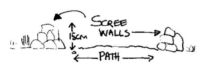

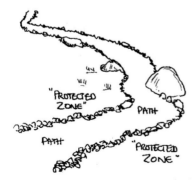

90 SCREE WALLS

RIPRAP

Where there is an abundance of loose stone it is possible to use RipRap in addition to scree walls. RipRap consists of loose stones placed over the entire surface restricting people to the more durable surfaces. RipRap is just tossed in a random fashion and makes walking difficult and therefore the footpath more inviting. RipRap is best used at steps (**Figure 91**) or to close off bootleg short cuts on switchbacks or where a new parallel path is tending to develop.

91 RipRap used at steps to stop walking or cycling to the side of the step which can lead to water damage.

92 USING THE NATURAL SHAPE OF THE LOG GIVES VERY EFFECTIVE PATH DEFINITION

ROCKS AND LOGS AS DEFINERS

Rocks and logs can be a very effective method of controlling trail spread in sensitive areas such as native woodland sites or biodiversity areas. Avoid straight lines or placing the rock or logs in too regular a fashion. Use the rock at bends and corners to emphasis the change in the trail as opposed to corralling the user along the trail. See Figures 92/93.

93 ROCKS USED AS TRAIL DEFINERS.
These locally sourced rocks make ideal definers for use in this woodland area and stop trail users from short cuts on the trail.

TRAIL BUILDER'S HINT
Keeping people on the trail is as much about psychology as it is about structures – good trail design and the subtle use of trail features such as RIP-RAP and scree walls can do more than fences and signs.

15. TRAIL CLEARANCE

TRAILS THROUGH WOODLAND AND FOREST

Trails and paths through woodlands should be free from any obstruction to walkers or hikers. All trails need to have clearance that allow unobstructed passage. As a rule the clearance should be a **mimimum of 1200mm wide by 2400mm high** for single file hiking trails and at least the width of the treadway for all other trails. **See Figure 94.**

Ensure that all trees adjacent to the trail are pruned with no stubs or 'coat hangers' left on the trail side of the tree as these can cause accidents to trail users. **See Figure 95.**

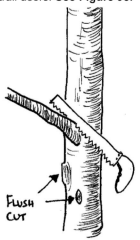

94 TRAIL CLEARANCE

95 FLUSH CUTS.
Cut the branch flush with the main stem. This ensures the tree can heal and that there are no eye hazards.

OPEN COUNTRY AND ENCROACHING VEGETATION

Furze, brambles and similar vegetation can cause walkers to move off the established tread way and thereby create bootleg trails. As a result trails through open land may require vegetation to be kept under control and cut back from time to time.

The vegetation on the upper side (**Figure 96**) of the trail should be cut back while the vegetation on the lower side (the side most prone to erosion) should be left to 'control' walkers and other trail users.

Over enthusiastic cutting should be avoided – hikers after all want to walk on a trail and not a motorway.

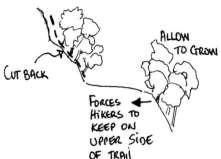

96 CUTTING BACK VEGETATION

16. SIGNAGE and TRAIL FURNITURE

Almost all trail networks will require some level of way-marking and signage. Unfortunately this can be one of the easiest things to do when creating a new trail and therefore all too often trail developers and promoters tend to concentrate on signage often to the detriment of tread way construction. Way-marking should reflect the level of usage; trails for experienced users will require less way-marking than trails that are designed to encourage the casual walker into the countryside.

There are various ways to mark trails from the standard way mark signs (Figure 97) approved by the **National Trails Office** (Irish Sports Council) for the use on national long distance trails, to the use of paint marks and cairns as is the tradition in many other countries. Whatever method you use, trail managers and developers should try and avoid over marking as the resultant signage pollution can take away from the recreation experience for all.

97 STANDARD WAY MARK POST

TRAIL HEAD SIGNS

Trailhead signs should be provided at car parks, trail heads and road crossings. Trailhead signs (**Figure 98**) orient the trail user and provide information that will aid their safe and enjoyable use of the trail. The information provided should include a **map**, important information on points of interest and hazards along the trail, rescue information, **regulations** (if they are in force) on camping, fire lighting, mountain biking etc. **Trail information** should include the **length of the trail**, the **grade of the trail** (for example - easy, moderate, strenuous) and the length of **time** it will take to walk or cycle for the average user. It is well worthwhile including the national Leave No Trace message to encourage better behaviour on the trails.

98 TRAILHEAD SIGN
Trailhead signs should ideally include a map, trail, safety and environmental information (Coillte standard design).

WAY-MARKING TRAILS

When marking trails it is essential to provide sufficient way-marking to ensure that users are confident in the route, but not too much such that signage pollution is a

problem. In **Figure 99** we have set out a schematic route-marking scheme. Way-marking must be provided at **all junctions** – in **both directions** – if it is a two-way trail. Use **'left / right'** way mark signs at a location on the junction where they are clearly visible from both directions.
Approximately **30m – 40m** from the junction provide a **'straight on'** sign to give reassurance that the walker is on the right trail having come through the junction. '**Straight on**' way mark signs should then be placed at approximately 5 -10 minutes (walking) intervals (400m – 600m) until the trail nears the next junction. At the next junction 'left/right' trails signs are required and a further reassurance sign after 30m - 40m and so on.

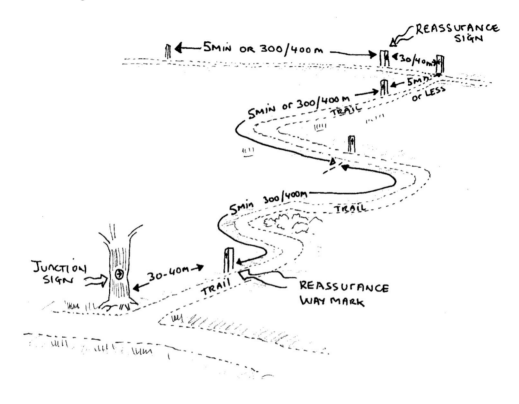

99 TYPICAL TRAIL WAY-MARKING SYSTEM

WAY-MARKING POSTS
The traditional way mark signs recommended by the National Trails Office are generally made from timber, recycled plastic or aluminium with a yellow arrow and walking man symbol. See **Figure 97.** The way-marking should be fixed at a height of between 1300mm and 1800mm (eye height).

FIX THE POST TO AVOID VANDALISM.
Ensure that all way mark posts are well set in the ground to discourage tampering. Use a sand/cement mix of **1-in-3**, which can be mixed dry and added to the small local rock and stone and tamped in around the post in the hole.

WAY-MARKING DISCS
A simpler method of way-marking trails is to use commercially available discs, which can be fitted to posts or trees along the route. Use **tamper proof screws** that cannot be removed with a

regular screwdriver. These way mark disc signs can also be fixed to rocks or similar surfaces with a proprietary adhesive such as Grip All or No More Nails.

PAINT MARKS AND CAIRNS

In more remote areas it is possible to use paint on rocks, boulders and trees as way-marking along the route. Ensure when using paint marks that other land managers marks, such as those used by harvesting foresters to mark timber harvests, are not using the same colour to mark their operations. Typically the marks should be about 150mm X 100mm (6 inches X 4 inches) in a rectangular or 150mm diameter if round shape. Make and use a template, for example a stencil cut from vinyl floor covering or similar material. This will ensure a consistent way mark symbol and will avoid the way mark sign looking like graffiti.

When marking a tree it may be necessary to remove some of the outer bark – conifer trees are often rough and should be scraped to remove the outer 'scales'. A paint scraper will be useful for this.

Adopt a **standard colour** for the trail and avoid using the same colour as other way marked trails that may cross your trail. Decide on a marking system and stick with that system along the entire length of the trail. Use **gloss paint** as it lasts longer than water-based paints; however, in Irish conditions these marks may need to be refreshed once a year.

100 PAINT TRAIL MARKING.
This trail marking in the Czech Republic is marking two different trails.

CAIRNS

In remote mountainous areas cairns (Figure 101) may be a good alternative to timber or plastic way mark posts. While there is not a tradition of marking mountain routes in Ireland, in Scotland and other countries the practice is used extensively to define routes. This helps limit trail spread and trampling.

Like any trail intervention, one needs to take care if using cairns as way markers. They should be used sparingly. Cairns should be kept small, less than 1000mm in height and constructed with care to discourage people's tendency to add to them. One other issue we need to consider before using cairns as way-markers in Ireland is that there are many cairns on the summits of Irish mountains – burial places from pre-history – which have to be respected and protected. Avoid doing anything that will cause stone to be removed from these cairns, many of which are national monuments and protected by law.

KEEP CAIRNS SMALL AND CONSTRUCT THEM WITH CARE TO DISCOURAGE OTHERS ADDING TO THEM. DO NOT TAKE STONE FROM NATIONAL MOUNUMENTS.

DISTANCE SIGNS

In Europe and the US it is common to provide trail information along the route particularly at junctions or important road crossings. These can be simple signs printed on plastic or metal or feature signs such as the more elaborate timber sign from Yosemite NP (Figure 102). They provide information on the **distance** in miles or kilometres to the next point of interest and can often include **time estimates for travel**. Some signs can include a Grid Reference or GPS position to aid navigation.

101 STONE CAIRNS

102 WOODEN DISTANCE SIGN giving the distance to the next point of interest.

FINGER POSTS

At developed parks, car parks and important access routes, finger posts can be used to give clear direction to the general trail users where the trail is heading e.g. 'car park' or 'mountain access route'.

STILES

All trails at one time or another will need to cross a wall or a fence. (Multi-access trails are of course the exception, as they cannot have an obstruction.) There are many types of stiles that can be bought from commercial manufacturers and these are made form a variety of materials including recycled plastics, timber and aluminium. The choice of stile will depend on the type and level of usage and of course the cost.

CONSTRUCTING YOUR OWN STILES

Alternatively, a stile may be constructed relatively easily using treated timber. Two simple stiles are illustrated here. For some other ideas for fence crossings see 'Fences, Gates and Bridges – a practical manual' (Details in Appendix III).

The first example illustrated (Figure 103) would typically be used to cross a fence or wall on a well-used trail with high numbers. This design can be purchased pre-fabricated in timber and aluminium.

The second example (Figure 104) is a simple stile construction and uses the strainer post of a fence line to support the ladder element. The strainer posts are usually at the corners of a fence

103 STANDARD 'FORESTRY' DESIGN STILE.

line or at approximately every 100m. Strainers are generally of a bigger dimension than a typical fencing post and are well set into the ground. Therefore they will support the ladder for crossing.

As with other timber structures ensure a good grip on the steps underfoot when wet. Ideally use staples left proud arranged in a pattern to give grip to the tread.

You can also use chicken wire fixed to the treads but this can rot over time and tends to collect mud and ice (during winter).

Some trail managers also use off cuts of chequer-plate steel (available from engineering works) but this can also trap moisture and speed up timber rot. Staples left proud of the step are the simplest, cheapest and best solution.

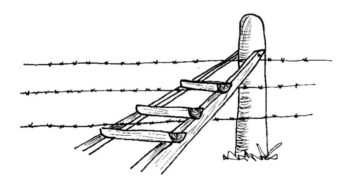

104 A SIMPLE UPLAND STILE.
This stile utilises the strainer post to support the ladder element. Ensure that the ladder is fixed to the strainer and not a run of the fence post.

HE IS ALL PINE AND I AM APPLE ORCHARD.

MY APPLES WILL NEVER GET ACROSS

AND EAT THE CONES UNDER HIS PINE, I TELL HIM.

HE ONLY SAYS, 'GOOD FENCES MAKE GOOD NEIGHBOURS'.

MENDING WALL.
ROBERT FROST

17. TOOLS

Having the right tools is essential to doing any job correctly. The basic tools for trail maintenance are the **mattock, crowbar, spade, shovel** and **pruning saw**. Moving materials will also require equipment such as much buckets, wheel-barrows or winches. All these with the exception of the mattock can be purchased easily in any hardware shop in Ireland.

TOOL CARE AND USE

Tools are safest when they are sharp and in good working order. Never use tools with loose or damaged heads and clean all tools before returning to the store. From a safety viewpoint it is best never to work alone. When working in a gang always keep a **safe working distance** from others (Figure 105).

SAFE WORKING DISTANCE
2 x HANDLES

105 SAFE WORKING CIRCLE

MATTOCK

The mattock (Figure 106) is probably the most versatile path maintainer's tool (and my favourite!). It is recommended as the **standard tool** for trail work.

The **pick end** can be used to loosen rocky, stony or very compacted soil. The broad flat end (the hoe head - circled) is used to rake out material from drains or holes and can also be used to cut roots or remove small stumps.

The edge of the tool can compact soil to form the treadway.

The head slides down over the handle from the user end and it is impossible for the dead to fly off.

If the head is loose it may be necessary to fix the head on the shaft of the handle with a screw just under the head.

SAFETY!

It is essential to keep at least two handle lengths away from others when using a mattock, pick or axe.

Check for adequate clearance **before** swinging a mattock or an axe. Remove any underbrush and overhanging branches that might interfere with, or catch, your swing.

Ensure stable and secure footing. Swing only when clear of other workers. Stand comfortably with your weight evenly distributed and both feet planted shoulder-width apart.

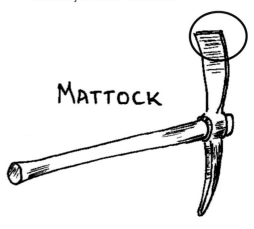

MATTOCK

106 PICK MATTOCK

PICKAXE
Similar to the mattock, it too can be used to loosen rocky, stony or compacted soil but is of little use to rake out material from drains, holes etc.

CROWBAR
These come in a variety of lengths, weights and with different ends. They can be used to move, loosen or prise heavy rocks. (See the text box on using the lever to move heavy rocks.) They are also used to create a lead hole for stakes and posts.

CROWBAR

> **SAFETY!**
> Take care to keep all fingers and feet out of the way when using a crowbar to prise rocks.

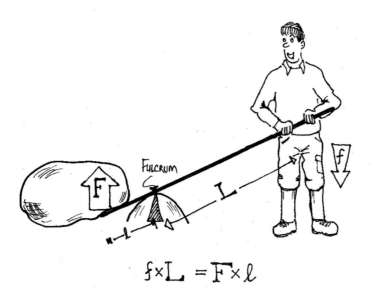

FULCRUM

F

L

f

$$f \times L = F \times \ell$$

107 THE POWER OF THE LEVER

USE THE POWER OF THE LEVER.
One of the basic laws of physics says that for 'every action there is an equal and opposite reaction'.

Trail maintainers can use this (law of the lever) very effectively to move heavy rock.

When trying to move a rock use a fulcrum (a rock) to give leverage to the bar.
The closer the **fulcrum** is to the rock being moved, the shorter the length (ℓ) of the crowbar from the fulcrum to the point of contact and the longer the length from the fulcrum to the user (**L**). (See Figure 107) The user is the source of the down ward force f.

The law of the lever means that $f \times L = F \times \ell$. The force downwards multiplied by the distance to the fulcrum equals the force upwards by the length from the fulcrum to the rock.

Therefore when pushed down, the force f will be changed to a much larger upward force **F** because the equation $f \times L = F \times \ell$ comes into play.

There a several types of spade – the one most suited to trail use is a small **planting spade** which has a short handle and small head. These are ideal for digging drains, cutting sods and general trail use.

SPADE

SHOVEL

SHOVEL
Shovels are used for shovelling loose material such as gravel, sand or aggregate. Shovels are not suitable for digging drains or similar cutting work. Chose a light shovel for trail work – they're lighter to carry to the work place.

THE GRIPE
Originally designed for use as a draining tool (hauling out sods from drains on bogs) we now use the gripe to haul sods and turfs for landscaping.

Safety: Take care when not using the GRIPE to ensure that the prongs are turned downward safely into the soil.

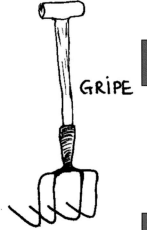

GRIPE

GLOVES AND GOGGLES
Gloves are essential when working with most materials especially rock and sharp stone. They guard against cuts and protect against splinters and thorns.
Goggles or safety glasses should always be used when breaking rock or trail clearing though woodlands to avoid eye injuries.

SAFETY!! Always remember to check the heads are secure on all sledges, hazel hoes, mattocks etc. before use and remember the safe working distance

SLEDGES AND MAULS
A sledge can be used to break rocks, drive stakes or tap steps and waterbars into place.

HAZEL HOE
Hazel hoes are similar to a mattock without the pick element. Their **wider head** make them ideal for cleaning drains and light landscaping work. The hazel hoe should not be used for heavy digging or rocky ground.

HAZEL HOE

SECATEURS AND LOPPERS

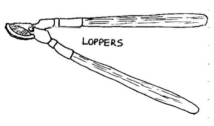

LOPPERS

Lopping and pruning shears are similar in design and use. Lopping shears have long handles and may have gears to increase leverage for thicker stems. Pruning shears are small enough to fit in one hand and are designed to cut small stems and branches. Cutting edges vary, but generally one blade binds and cuts a stem against an anvil or bevelled hook. Lopping and pruning shears do a better job than hand saws by making a nice clean cut when removing branches. Wear gloves and <u>always cut the branch flush with the main stem.</u>

SAWS

PRUNING SAWS are useful for brashing and can be used for removing small blow-downs, especially where space is limited and cutting is difficult. All pruning saws should come with a scabbard or a folding mechanism. Folding pruning saws are handy and suitable for trail maintenance volunteers as they can be easily stored in rucksacks.

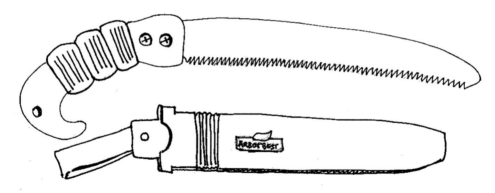

BOW SAWS

For larger dimension timber a **bow saw** is ideal and will get through the timber almost as quickly as a chain saw (and is more environmentally friendly.) The trick with all sawing is to maintain a **relaxed and even stroke**. Pull the saw towards you and don't push or the saw will buckle and stick.

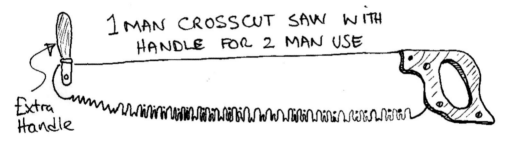

1 MAN CROSSCUT SAW WITH HANDLE FOR 2 MAN USE

Extra Handle

CROSSCUT SAWS are designed for a sawyer at either end. They follow two basic patterns. **Felling crosscuts** are light and flexible. **Bucking** or crosscut saws have straight backs and are heavier and stiffer than felling saws. Crosscut saws are recommended for most trail work because they are more versatile. Volunteers can use crosscut saws to cut large blow-downs that may block trails after storms, like bow saws they are more environmentally sound and also safer for volunteer use.

SAW CARE
Keep the saw covered and sheathed when not in use. Oil or spray with WD40 to keep them rust free when storing. Keep a good blade on your saw; it's much easier to saw with a sharp blade. Blades for bow saws only cost a few Euros, so keep a new one handy.

Take care when carrying the saw to and from the worksite – keep the saw blade covered and guarded. When using the saw wear gloves to avoid skinning knuckles.

CHAINSAWS

> **SAFETY!!**
> **Don't allow volunteers to use chainsaws unless they have a certificate of competence from a training agency.**
> **Most landowners in Ireland now require a certificate of competency to operate a chainsaw on their land – check the landowner requirements.**
> **Contact a qualified chain saw training provider to obtaining training and assessment of competency.**

THE MCLEOD combines a heavy-duty rake with a large, sturdy hoe. McLeods work well for constructing trails through light soils and vegetation or for re-establishing the tread when material from the back slope falls onto the trail.
A McLeod is useful for compacting tread and trail builders use the handle for checking out slope. McLeods are inefficient in rocky or unusually brushy areas.

THE MC LEOD

CLINOMETER
A clinometer is a simple, yet useful, instrument for measuring slopes or grades. Most clinometers have two scales, one indicating **percent of slope**, the other showing the slope in **degrees**. A clinometer is very useful when laying out a trail to get the gradient of side slopes and the gradient of trails. Both of these are essential to getting the correct route and estimating the spacing distance of water management features. (**See Appendix I – Gradients**)

MOVING MATERIALS
Moving materials on site safely and efficiently is essential to good trail work (and happy crews!) Several non-mechanical methods can be used including buckets, barrows, timber tongs and winches.

MUCK BUCKET

Moving soil, gravel etc on a work site can often be difficult given the nature of the terrain.

A muck bucket, which is made from flexible plastic, is the most durable tool for this purpose. Ideally two people use them and lifting can be made easier by passing a shovel handle through the bucket handles and gripping this instead of the bucket handles.

Muck Buckets can be purchased in most garden centres.

MUCK BUCKET

TIMBER TONGS

Timber tongs are ideal for moving logs. The tongs grip the log when lifted by the handle (Figure 108) and are easily released when the log is put down. Timber tongs can be purchase from most chain saw retailers.

TIMBER TONGS

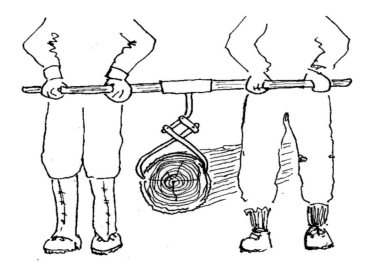

108 TIMBER TONGS

It is possible to buy larger tongs or to modify single-handed tongs so they can be used by two people (Figure 109). Timber tongs used in this way are a safe and efficient way of moving larger logs.

109 TIMBER TONGS
These can be modified in an engineering works to allow a timber handle to be fitted thereby allowing two people to lift with ease.

WINCHES

Winches or Grip hoists are ideal for moving heavy weights such as large boulders or logs at a work site.

The winch is simply operated by a back and forth movement, which engages a one-way gearing system and slowly but surely moves the heavy object towards the winch. The winch must be securely anchored to a good ground anchor, boulder or tree – take care not to damage the tree.

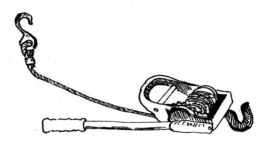

110 RATCHET WINCH

111 THE DANGER ZONE FOR A RATCHET WINCH.
The danger zone is marked YELLOW.

WINCH SAFETY

The area between the winch and the load is the danger zone (Figure 111). The cable is under tension and could cause serious injury should it snap accidentally.
Keep this area clear of all people when the winch is in use.
Most winches are fitted with handles that will bend or snap when the load is too great thereby avoiding catastrophic wire break.

Always use the correct manufacturers handle and avoid at all costs using an unspecified replacement handle – anything else is unsafe.

While winches are simple to operate they do require some basic training before use and always pay attention to basic safety.

TOOL MAINTENANCE

Finally – well-maintained tools make working safer, easier, effective and more fun.

Appoint a <u>quartermaster</u> and do a regular tool check and maintenance at least once a year preferably before the tools are put away for the winter.

- Check that all handles are sound. Replace any damaged or worn parts such as handles, saw blades etc.
- Clean and oil wooden handles with linseed oil before long storage.
- Clean all metal parts of tools before storing, removing dirt with a wire brush and oil lightly with an aerosol oil spray.
- Make sure all cutting surfaces are clean, sharp, oiled and sheathed for the winter.
- Equipment like ratchet winches should be cleaned, checked for damage, repaired, oiled and greased before storage.

LOOK AFTER TOOLS – THEY ARE COSTLY!

TRAIL CLEARANCE

18. VOLUNTEERING FOR TRAILS

BUILDING A TRAIL COMMUNITY

Developing a culture of trail work within the outdoor recreation community takes time. People should not be shamed, embarrassed or badgered into joining the effort. As people get used to seeing trail work they'll realise that now and in the future it will be an inherent part of being a hiker, mountain biker and outdoors person. In Mountain Meitheal we believe that trail work is another outdoor activity that people can get enjoyment and satisfaction from. If already involved, keep organising workdays and inviting others to join, if not, maybe it's time to start.

SWEAT EQUITY

In the final analysis volunteers may never turn out in huge numbers, but those that do are generating sweat equity in their favourite recreation area. This in time will mean that they can have a say in how these areas are managed and protected.

Trail maintenance organisations need to seek out those who are interested in performing trail work and convincing them to give it a go.

VOLUNTEERING FOR TRAILS

Trail management is a costly business and although the major landowners such as the National Park Service and Coillte (The Irish Forestry Board) spend considerable amounts on our national network of trails it is simply not enough. In other countries volunteers undertake trail work – often supporting the work of professional crews – making a real contribution to conserving the environment by maintaining the trail network.

In Mountain Meitheal we are attempting to counteract some of the pressures that are evident on our mountains by working with the various landowners such as Coillte, The Dublin Mountains Partnership, The National Park and Wildlife Service and private landowners.

GETTING AND KEEPING VOLUNTEERS (.....HAPPY!!)

One of the most challenging aspects facing trail maintenance clubs and trail managers is attracting volunteers to help with trail construction and maintenance. Many people lack the confidence to make a start – they think the work will be too hard, they don't have the skills or that they will be drummed into stuff that doesn't interest them.
Here are some ideas that may help attract and keep volunteers:

LETTING EVERYONE KNOW

The first challenge facing any group is one of awareness. Encourage people to participate by making them aware of the work or project being undertaken.

Information can be disseminated in many ways. When starting up a group, the traditional way is through posters and articles in local newspapers and outdoor magazines. Posters at forest and mountain car parks or at local outdoor shops announcing the particulars of trail work days will help to attract volunteers. Hand out flyers at car parks announcing your trail work project. Invite walking or bike clubs to join your club for a workday. Announcements on local radio can increase exposure as well.

10 STEPS TO HELP GETTING A VOLUNTEER GROUP STARTED

112 Keep it simple in the beginning. This trail hut constructed by Mountain Meitheal took considerable planning before the actual workday.

Ten tips that will help you get started on creating a successful volunteer effort.

PREPARATION

1. First decide on the project. Keep it simple in the beginning.
Make a list of some simple goals and keep the project relatively short (in time) and basic. List all the actions that you need to complete before starting including meeting with the land owner/manager, getting the word out to potential volunteers, getting a specification for the work, organising the tools etc.

Estimate how much time it will take and how many volunteers will be needed to complete each project, this will help you ensure you don't bite off more than you or your group can chew.

2. Get help.
Find others to help spread the workload of setting up the volunteer group. At least two to three committed people are required to start up a group. Delegate the workload – no one person can do it all and burnout is a distinct possibility if you try. Develop a good back-up plan. The ultimate aim should be to develop a group of crew leaders that can take over when needed.

3. Be Strategic.
Do something that will be worthwhile – not work for works sake. Develop a simple programme for a few months, which allows for advance notice. Whether it is once a year (on NATIONAL TRAILS DAY might be a good start), once a month (like the 3rd Saturday) or once a week (every Sunday), predictability will help people plan their involvement. Use local shops, petrol stations, libraries and trail head signboards to place notices for the workday. Use other club event calendars, community or other web sites to get the word out.
If people are interested, set up an email list to remind people.

4. Invite a friend to join you.

THE WORK DAY
5. Structure the day. A successful trail workday has these 3 ingredients:

• **Enjoyment.** Don't take it too seriously, use a little humour, and encourage friendly competition and a social element afterwards – regroup at the local pub or café for a pint or coffee and a chat.

- **Education.** Teach new skills and demonstrate new tools. More seasoned volunteers can help with this and take new volunteers under their wing.

- **Accomplishment**. Match crew leaders and their groups to tasks that are within their capacity and the time available. Avoid leaving a job half-finished or rushing at the end. The trail must be safe for volunteers and other trail users after you leave.

6. Communication is the key on the workday. Start with introductions by the crew leaders, and the individuals (particularly if the group is new). Remind people to sign up, run through a safety briefing (**tool talk**) and outline the day's format. Count heads and assign crew leaders.

7. Place signs to notify others of your work.
Place notices at the trailhead and at the work site to promote safety, give credit to your team's efforts, and encourage others to join in on the day or attend the next work party.
Don't let your volunteers harass or embarrass other trail users who come by. Be positive and encourage them to help out next time. Offer a copy of the club's newsletter or an information sheet.

8. Be a good supervisor.
Working alongside the volunteers **is important**, but keeping the work flowing safely, providing encouragement and monitoring progress **is essential**.

Give clear instructions and explain the standards and specifications so volunteers and crew leaders can understand the 'why' and the 'how' of the work at hand.
Make notes and take photographs of the project, especially 'before and after' shots. These are useful for the project record, newsletters and reports.

THE FOLLOW UP
9. Provide recognition.
Everyone likes to know they are appreciated so make sure to thank volunteers for coming out on the day. Provide a souvenir, such as a club badge or club pin or a T-shirt to remind them of the day. Afterwards, write up the event in the club newsletter or annual report. Mountain Meitheal has an end of year slide show at our annual Christmas dinner where volunteers are featured working during the year. Recognise top volunteers at the club's year-end celebration. The sign-up sheets and notes will help to give credit where credit is due.

10. Keep good records.
It is very important to keep good records of the time you put into the project preparation, the events of the day itself, and the number of **volunteers/hours generated**. This information will help in planning the next project, and **can be used to show the club's commitment and generate that sweat equity**. Grant applications for funding are stronger when they demonstrate a track record of volunteer projects. Share this information, trail work hours and metres of trails opened, to build credibility for all outdoor users.

UP AND RUNNING
Once a group is established, to collect and build an email database. Mountain Meitheal uses e-mail messages to inform all its members and supporters of events and workdays. Have volunteers sign up each day. Get their names, addresses, phone numbers and e-mail addresses, then follow up and keep them involved. This is particularly important with a new, first-time volunteer.
IF A FIRST-TIME VOLUNTEER HAS ENOUGH INTEREST TO SHOW UP ONCE, THEY WILL MOST LIKELY RETURN IF THEY LEAVE FEELING WELCOMED AND APPRECIATED.

Mountain Meitheal has also developed a web site and a newsletter to communicate information on its activities to members, friends and supporters. Develop a calendar of trail work and post it on your website – this allows volunteers to plan their work days to suit their other commitments.

TRAIN CREW LEADERS

Train your crew leaders in trail construction techniques and crew leading. Mountain Meitheal and the National Trails Office offer trail building courses from time to time.

If you don't have any trained crew leaders keep the work simple and see if you can train a few of your members.

Keep your crew leaders up to date relating to what work their crew will be doing. Have a clear specification (See page 83) so crew leaders know what they have to do.

LOOK AFTER THE TROOPS!

VOLUNTEERS NEED TO KNOW THEY ARE APPRECIATED. We can't emphasise this enough! A big 'THANK YOU' goes a long way. List volunteers in newsletter articles, post photos of workers on your group's web site.

Mountain Meitheal rewards volunteers who have worked 30 or more hours with a special club fleece. A summer BBQ and a party at Christmas is held to recognize volunteers contribution and allow everyone to socialise and clap themselves on the back.

Some groups give out special t-shirts, fleeces, caps, badges or awards for exceptional effort.

ONE LAST THING

Don't take it too seriously. Remember to have fun, keep it interesting, and help others make a difference. Go for it and good luck!

'GET OUT, GET DIRTY, GIVE BACK'

19. A FEW WORDS FOR CREW LEADERS

LEADERSHIP

'They lead best who seem to lead least'.
Sun Tsu, a Chinese philosopher, over 2000 years ago.

Good leaders provide the means for people to do good work and at the same time give them the feeling that 'we did it ourselves'. While styles of leadership may vary, effective leaders share the following qualities.

They ensure a safe working environment for their crews and themselves. They have the right and responsibility of ultimate decision-making. Establish ground rules at the start of the workday and insist they are followed. Good leaders clearly communicate their expectations.

PLANNING, PLANNING, AND PLANNING

Obtain permissions (SAC permits and felling licences etc. – see Chapter 4 Getting started on the ground) and agreements from the land owner/manager.

Ensure that you have the right tools for the job on the day and that they are in good repair. Many trail groups set up a tool store and put someone in charge of maintaining it.

Ensure you have the agreed work specification for the project. (See Table 6, Specification).

Prioritise tasks so you can focus on what needs to be done regardless of the turnout. Don't work people to death or waste their time; remember they are there to enjoy their day and all have different abilities and expectations.

CREW SIZE AND WORK DAY LENGTH

A crew of **eight to twelve people is ideal**. Break the crew into groups of four to five volunteers and put an experienced volunteer with each group. Ensure everyone knows what he or she is supposed to be doing. Meet at **10.30,** be on site by **11.00** and finish about **16.00–16.30**. Work for no more than **five to six hours** – remember many of these people do not work physically in their day job. This is a reasonable commitment for your average volunteer.

TRAIL SPECIFICATION
MOUNTAIN MEITHEAL

TRAIL: *Deer park trail from grid reference O 112 986 to O 113 101 ; approximately 350m in length.*

GENERAL DESCRIPTION OF WORK:
Repair trail with drainage, water bars and the addition of Rip-Rap to stop short cutting off trail. This trail crosses a very wet section roughly in the middle which will require the construction of some rustic bog bridges over sections. Timber can be brought onto the site along the forest road which comes within 50m of the trail at grid reference O 112 122.

MARKER POINTS	DIST.	SPECIFICATION / INSTRUCTIONS
1 on Rt Just below waterbar near gate exiting the forest.	0m	From 1-2 clear any loose stones and place in the corner to the left of (1) as RipRap. (See page 59 of MM guide for details of RipRap)
2 on Rt	+ 80m	Finish drain at the wall to connect to main drain at 1 From 2-3 take the stones from the side of the path (scree wall at present) and put on right hand side of path in the existing drain as Rip-Rap to slow down water flow.
3 on left	+ 20m	@ 3 Put sump at outfall of the current waterbar to slow down water flow. 3-4 Move the stones from the side of the path (as scree wall at present) and put on right hand side of path in the existing drain as Rip-Rap to slow down water flow.
4L	+ 25m	Construct _stone_ waterbar just below large rock at 120° to the main trail. (See page 48 of MM guide for details of stone waterbars)
5L	+25m	Construct _stone_ waterbar at 120° to the main trail. Put stone into right hand drain to slow down water. Landscape left hand side of trail and aim for path width of 1.4-1.5m
6R		Construct _stone_ waterbar at 120° to the main trail. 5-7 Put stone into right hand drain to slow down water. Move big rocks onto path to act as trail definers.

TABLE 6 EXAMPLE OF A WORK SPECIFICATION

CREW LEADERS SHOULD REMEMBER......

- First, all our workers are volunteers – they are there to do some worthwhile work while having a good day out.

- Treat people with respect, listen to their views but be clear and firm on matters of safety and work objectives.

- Don't ask some one to do something you are not prepared to do yourself.

- Don't assume that what a leader can do, everyone else can do – they can't.

- Absolutely no sarcastic or bullying remarks and don't tolerate such behaviour from others.

- In Ireland, countryside access politics can be divisive; best avoid it and leave all such discussions at the trailhead. Mountain Meitheal has clear objectives – they maybe the only things we share in common. Our objectives are all we can expect people to sign up to. If you are starting a new group ensure your group has clear (written) objectives.

- Speak to other mountain and path users about your work with courtesy and enthusiasm. As trail volunteers, we only have the 'authority of the resource' but that's very powerful.

- **ABOVE ALL, ENJOY THE EXPERIENCE.**

CHECKLIST FOR YOUR WORK DAY

Plan – Have you a plan for the work? Develop a specification for the site. (See above).

Permission – Have you the Landowners permission and necessary licences? (See **Getting started**, Chapter 4).

Materials – Are these available and suitable?

Tools – You will need to organise collection and transport of the tools to the work site.

Notified all crew members? – Have you notified everyone about the day? Email is a great way.

First aid kit – Have one available on site and ensure that some one can use it!

Access – Do need a key to access the site?

Carry out hazard identification. This should be done as part of the overall plan. (See **Safety,** Chapter 2). Post the hazard identification at the work site.

Safety (toolbox) talk – The crew leader should give a concise safety talk before work starts, outlining the work for the day, types of tools the crew will be using and any potential hazards.

Leave the site clean and safe after you finish each workday.

Thank the volunteers for their efforts. (Hand out badges and or an application form to new volunteers).

Clean and return tools to store or the temporary storage.

Report on the day to your club and the landowner.

AND FINALLY – THE LAST TEN PERCENT

Don't forget the last ten percent. Pay attention to details, the cleanup of the site after the work is finished and the care of the tools make a great difference to all projects. Leaders should **include time for the last ten percent** and motivate gangs to take pride in giving their work the polish it deserves.

TAKE YOUR PICK

Trail work can be a most enjoyable and rewarding activity in the outdoors. Some people walk, some climb, some mountain bike and now more and more people build trails and get involved in trail conservation. If you would like to get involved, it's easy, all it requires is a little determination and a few like-minded people. By joining in this effort you will be joining with many other hundreds and thousands around the world who care about their environment and give the time and enthusiasm to do something about it.

So, Come Out, Get Dirty, Give Back,

Mountain Meitheal

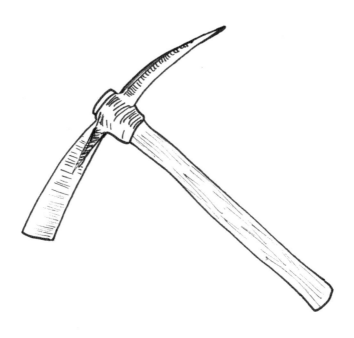

APPENDIX I Gradients for Use in Trail Construction

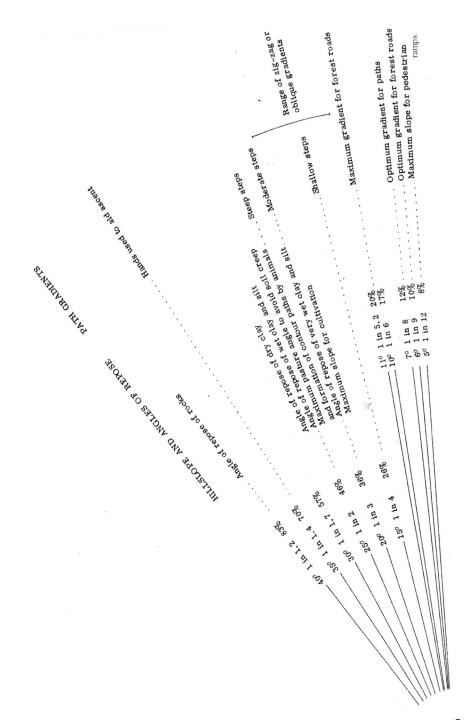

Appendix II   Walking and Hiking Trail Classes

CLASS 1 - WALKING TRAIL	
GENERAL DESCRIPTION	• Specifically multi-access trails which can accommodate users with reduced mobility. • Will be serviced by a vehicle parking area. • Allows two-way traffic. • No steps, waterbars, stiles, barriers or trip hazards of any kind. • Should have resting places with seating approximately every 100m.
SITE SUITABILITY	Urban/Urban Fringe or Core Recreation Areas but some trails providing access to reduced mobility users may also be appropriate in other areas.
TRAIL SURFACE	Sealed non-slip surfaces, timber boardwalk, tarmac or compacted surface with no loose stone or gravel greater than 5mm.
TRAIL WIDTH	Desirable: 2500mm. Minimum: 1800mm
TRAIL GRADIENT	Flat 0% – 5% Maximum: up to 9% allowed for ramps where required

Note: National Trail Standards.
These trail guidelines are the national standards developed by the national trails office and detailed in their trail standards available on-line from

http://www.irishtrails.ie/National_Trails_Office/Publications/Management_Standards.pdf

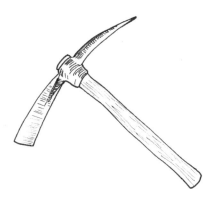

CLASS 2 - WALKING TRAIL	
GENERAL DESCRIPTION	• Essentially trails for casual use, serviced by a vehicle parking area • Reasonably flat and wide enough to accommodate two-way traffic. • Will have a relatively smooth surface with minimal loose material. • Stiles should be kept to a minimum. Steps should be minimal and if used should be limited. • May use bridges and boardwalks, which should have resting places with seating approximately every 500m.
SITE SUITABILITY	Urban/Urban Fringe or Core Recreation Areas or Rural landscapes/forests
TRAIL SURFACE	Consistent sealed surfaces, timber boardwalk or compacted aggregate – 20mm to dust stone.
TRAIL WIDTH	Range: Minimum: 1200mm – 2000mm Desirable: 1800mm
TRAIL GRADIENT	Range 0% – 8% Desirable 5%

Note: National Trail Standards.
These trail guidelines are the national standards developed by the national trails office and detailed in their trail standards available on-line from
http://www.irishtrails.ie/National_Trails_Office/Publications/Management_Standards.pdf

CLASS 3 - WALKING TRAIL	
GENERAL DESCRIPTION	• Typically relatively narrow undulating trails • Will have moderate gradients. • Surface may be variable including loose material and can be uneven in places. • May include steps, protruding roots and rocks, waterbars, stiles and gates. • May include bog bridges and boardwalks
SITE SUITABILITY	Core Recreation Areas or Rural landscapes/forests
TRAIL SURFACE	Variable surfaces including some loose material not greater than 50mm in size
TRAIL WIDTH	Range: 600mm –1200mm Desirable: 800mm – 1000mm
TRAIL GRADIENT	Range: flat to Maximum 12% Desirable: 5%

CLASS 4 - WALKING TRAIL	
GENERAL DESCRIPTION	• Typically challenging, single file walking trails over mixed terrain. • May have steep gradients. • Surface will be very variable and may include loose material, steps, protruding roots and rocks, waterbars, stiles and gates. • Trail types include aggregate, stone pitched.
SITE SUITABILITY	Rural landscapes/forests or Upland and Remote
TRAIL SURFACE	Very variable and uneven surfaces including loose material up to 100mm in size; protruding roots and rocks.
TRAIL WIDTH	Range: 500mm – 1000mm Desirable 800mm
TRAIL GRADIENT	Range: Flat to Maximum 30% Desirable: 10%

CLASS 5 - WALKING TRAIL	
GENERAL DESCRIPTION	• Challenging trails, surfaced or unsurfaced, over variable ground
SITE SUITABILITY	Upland or Remote areas
TRAIL SURFACE	• Can include rough steps, stiles, waterbars, side drain, simple bridges or river crossings • Extremely variable and uneven surfaces with large rocks, roots and other obstacles offering a challenging hike.
TRAIL WIDTH	Range: 500mm – 1000mm Desirable: 800mm
TRAIL GRADIENT	No gradient constraints Desirable: Maximum 40% requiring steps

Note: National Trail Standards.
These trail guidelines are the national standards developed by the national trails office and detailed in their trail standards available on-line from
http://www.irishtrails.ie/National_Trails_Office/Publications/Management_Standards.pdf

APPENDIX III CYCLING TRAIL CLASSES

CLASS 1 – OFF-ROAD CYCLING TRAIL	
GENERAL DESCRIPTION	• Flat trails intended for family use by all ages and all types of bikes including children's bikes with stabilisers. • Wide enough to accommodate two-way usage. • Even consistent sealed surface with no trail features[5] or obstacles. • Has low gradient to ensure slow speeds and safe use in any direction. • May use bridges and boardwalks *Typically suitable in:* Urban/ Urban Fringe or Core Recreation Areas
TRAIL SURFACE	Consistent sealed surfaces, or compacted material. Minimal loose material no larger than 6mm.
TRAIL WIDTH	Minimum: 2500mm Boardwalk or bridges – minimum: 2000mm
TRAIL GRADIENT	Average: 3%. Maximum: 5%

CLASS 2 – OFF-ROAD CYCLING TRAIL	
GENERAL DESCRIPTION	• Small gradients but essentially level trails to ensure slow speeds and travel in any direction. • Wide enough to accommodate two-way usage. • Very minor grade reversals but no other trail features can be included. • Will be suitable for bikes with tag-a-longs, but not bikes with stabilisers or child seats. • May use bridges and boardwalks • Typically gravel roads and suitable purpose built trails. *Typically suitable in:* Urban/Urban Fringe or Core Recreation areas
TRAIL SURFACE	Consistent sealed surfaces, or compacted material. Minimal loose material no larger than 20mm.
TRAIL WIDTH	Minimum: 1800mm
TRAIL GRADIENT	Average: 5%. Maximum 5% downhill; 10% uphill.

---

[5] A trail feature is a step, drop or grade reversal

Note: National Trail Standards.

CLASS 3 – OFF-ROAD CYCLING TRAIL	
GENERAL DESCRIPTION	• Moderate gradients and narrower trails suitable for use in one direction only. • Wide steep descents must not be included. • Require a basic level of competency in bike control. • Suitable for mountain bikes only. • May include some uneven surfaces with unavoidable obstacles or rock steps and protruding rocks and roots. *Typically suitable in:* Core Recreation Areas or Rural landscapes/forests
TRAIL SURFACE	Variable and slightly uneven surfaces including some loose material not greater than 50mm in size. Rock steps of not more than 60mm and protruding rocks and roots no more than 40mm above the trail surface.
TRAIL WIDTH	Minimum: 1000mm Boardwalk or bridges – minimum: 1200mm, not raised more than 300mm above the surface of the ground. Bridges must have handrails throughout.
TRAIL GRADIENT	Average 8%; Maximum: 8% downhill; 15% uphill

CLASS 4 – OFF-ROAD CYCLING TRAIL	
GENERAL DESCRIPTION	• These are technically challenging trails, which require high levels of competency in bike control and a high level of physical fitness. • Can include tight turns of up to 180 degrees, unavoidable rock steps, protruding roots and rocks. • May be narrow and tight and wide steep descents must not be used. • These trails should be used in one direction only • Not suitable for children under 11 years of age. *Typically suitable in:* Rural landscapes/forests or Upland and Remote
TRAIL SURFACE	Very variable and uneven surfaces including loose material up to 100mm in size; protruding roots and rocks and rock steps up to 150mm high.
TRAIL WIDTH	Not less than 600mm Boardwalk not less than 600mm wide and not more than 1500mm above the ground. Bridges should be not less than 1000mm and if more than 1500mm high, should have hand rails.
TRAIL GRADIENT	Average 10%; Maximum 25% downhill; 20% uphill

CLASS 5 – OFF-ROAD CYCLING TRAIL	
GENERAL DESCRIPTION	• Extremely technically and physically challenging trails requiring high levels of competency in bike control and a high level of physical fitness. • These trails should be very narrow and tight, with extremely demanding gradients • These trails will have very large features and should be used in one direction only • Suitable for children over 14 years of age and mountain bikes with suspension only. **Typically suitable in:** *Upland or Remote areas (see table 3.1)*
TRAIL SURFACE	Extremely variable and uneven surfaces with large loose rocks, boulders and roots up to 100mm. Rock steps of up to 600mm in height, protruding roots and rocks of up to 300mm.
TRAIL WIDTH	Minimum: 300mm Boardwalk width minimum 600mm
TRAIL GRADIENT	Average 15%; 50% maximum downhill; 25% maximum uphill

Note: National Trail Standards.
These trail guidelines are the national standards developed by the national trails office and detailed in their trail standards available on line from
http://www.irishtrails.ie/National_Trails_Office/Publications/Management_Standards.pdf

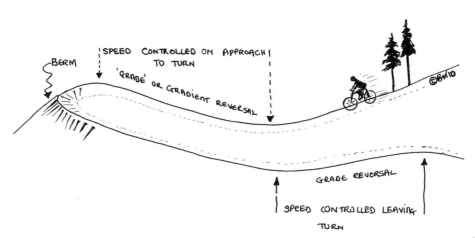

APPENDIX IV RESOURCES –
Books, Guides, Websites and Suppliers

'The complete guide to trail building and maintenance' - Appalachian Mountain Club
This is an excellent primer, used by US Forest Service and others. It's available from the club website or from www.amazon.com.

'Appalachian Trail Field book - Maintenance and Rehabilitation Guidelines for Volunteers'
- Appalachian Trail Conservancy.
This is an excellent little handbook in a very handy format. It is available from the Appalachian Trail Conservancy web site bookshop.

'Appalachian trail, design, construction and maintenance'.
Appalachian Trail Conservancy
This is a good guide with many interesting asides. It has a strong emphasis on low impact solutions. Available from the Appalachian Trail Conservancy and Amazon

'Lightly on the land - the SCA trail building and maintenance manual.' - Student
Conversation Association website and published by Mountaineer Books.
This is an excellent guide to trail work with a strong environmental emphasis. This book has simple easily understood solutions and good line drawings. Available from www.amazon.com.

'Guidelines for the Developing and Marking of Way-marked Ways'
Published by the Irish Sports Council and the Heritage Council. Covers many of the issues encountered in establishing a way marked route – Available from the National Trails Office (See website details below). (This is an Irish Publication)

'Management standards for recreation trails'
This is an excellent book giving clearly defined standards for Irish trails.
Published by the National Trails Office easily available as a download PDF from www.irishtrails.ie (An Irish Publication)

'Classification and grading for recreation trails'
When trails managers talk about a class III trail what do they mean? This book gives dimensions, gradients etc. for use on Irish Trails. Published by the National Trails Office. (An Irish Publication)

BOOKS CONTINUED

'Irish Trails Strategy' Published by the National Trails Office.

Available as a download PDF from www.irishtrails.ie (An Irish Publication)

'Trail Planning and Development Guide', 2011

Published by the National Trails Office – available as a download PDF from www.irishtrails.ie (An Irish Publication)

'Trail Solutions. IMBA's Guide to Building Sweet Singletrack'

This is an excellent guide for mountain bikers wanting to build sustainable trails.

Available from the IMBA website or Amazon.com

'A guide to log lean-to construction', – Maine Appalachian Trail Club.

Available from Amazon.com. This is a good guide to trail hut design and construction and useful for those interested in developing simple overnight shelters.

'Repairing upland path erosion – a best practice guide'

Published by the National Trust and English Nature.

This is a good guide with lots of solutions but diagrams can be a little hard to follow. As this is a guide from the UK the terrain and issues are similar to ours – the book does have good photos.

'Footpaths – a practical handbook', Elizabeth Agate

Published by BTCV publications, Available on web site.

'Natural Surface Trails by Design – Physical and Human Design Essentials of Sustainable Enjoyable Trails', Troy Scott Parker.

Published by www.natureshape.com. This is an interesting book and the first of a series that the author is publishing.

'Trail Design for small properties', Mel Baughman & Terry Serres

Published by the University of Minnesota Extension Service. Available online

This is a short booklet with good clear text and diagrams.

'Fences, Gates and Bridges – a practical manual'

Published by Alan C. Hood and Company. Available from amazon.com

This is a reprint of a book first published in 1887 with lots of diagrams giving ideas on fencing, bridges etc. One for the trail anoraks!

USEFUL GEAR SOURCES

www.benmeadows.com – A US based forestry and outdoors supplies company. Everything you need for trail work from flagging tape and measuring wheels to mattocks and directional markers. They have a speedy and efficient service, but you will have to pay customs charges – despite this, gear can still work out at a very good price.

www.forestrysuppliers.com – Another US based forestry and outdoors supplies company. More of everything you need. Speedy service and customs charges will also apply.

Woodies, B & Q, Homebase. Warehouses carry reasonably priced shovels, spades, muck buckets and other outdoor tools.

Lidl and **Aldi** often carry garden equipment such as pruning saws and loppers at very reasonable prices.

USEFUL WEBSITES TRAIL BUILDERS

www.appalachiantrail.org APPALACHIAN TRAIL CONSERVANCY – links to many trail repair clubs along the eastern United States that build and maintain trails.

www.btcv.org.uk – British Conservation Volunteers – a useful source of information and gear. They also offer volunteer holidays

www.pathsavers.org – Mountain Meitheal's own website with links, programme of work days and useful information in the Irish context.

www.outdoors.org APPALACHIAN MOUNTAIN CLUB – lots of contacts and links to path conservation issues including courses.

www.thesca.org The Student Conservation Association – A US based conservation organisation for younger adults with information on events and volunteering opportunities.

www.MATC.org The Maine Appalachian Trail Club maintains over 127 miles of the AT in Maine. Our neighbours across the pond.

www.imba.com The international Mountain Biking Association – lots of good information on developing sustainable mountain bike trails and dealing with landowners.

USEFUL WEBSITES GENERAL

www.coillteoutdoors.ie – Coillte's dedicated recreation website provides lots of information on trails, outdoor recreation and useful hints for those heading to the outdoors.
Over 250 trails are listed along with special features and activities.

www.irishtrails.ie – The website of the National Trails Office is an important resource for anyone considering developing a trail in Ireland. It has information on the national trail standards, classification and grades and also provides information on getting started on trail development. This website also hosts details of trails on the national trails register and other information valuable for trail work in Ireland.

www.nationaltrailsday.ie – Now a fixture in the annual calendar National Trails Day celebrates Irelands trail network

www.leavenotraceireland.org –The Irish LEAVE NO TRACE website promoting responsible outdoor recreation – information on how to join, training, forum, news etc.